The Academic Job
Search Handbook

The Academic Job Search Handbook

Mary Morris Heiberger
and Julia Miller Vick

upp

UNIVERSITY OF PENNSYLVANIA PRESS   Philadelphia

Library of Congress Cataloging-in-Publication Data

Heiberger, Mary Morris.
    The academic job search handbook / Mary Morris Heiberger and Julia
Miller Vick.
        p.   cm.
    Includes bibliographical references (p.) and index.
    ISBN 0-8122-1375-0
    1. College teachers—Employment—United States—Handbooks,
manuals, etc.   2. College teachers—United States—Selection and
appointment—Handbooks, manuals, etc.   I. Vick, Julia Miller.
II. Title.
LB2331.72.H45   1992
378.1'2'02373—dc20   91-42531
                                                                                        CIP

Contents

Acknowledgments

The first version of this handbook was written in consultation with our original Graduate Faculty Placement Council, an advisory group to the University of Pennsylvania's Career Planning and Placement Service. Its members contributed their vast experience to and carefully commented on the document.

We thank all those who first served as members of the Graduate Faculty Placement Council: Dr. Beth E. Allen, Economics; Dr. Elijah Anderson, Sociology; Dr. Fred L. Block, Sociology; Dr. Lee V. Cassanelli, History; Dr. Peter Conn, English; Dr. Terry H. Fortune, Physics; Dr. Stephen Gale, Regional Science; Dr. Marcia I. Lester, Chemistry; Ms. Maggie Morris, Graduate Division, School of Arts and Sciences; Dr. Edward N. Pugh, Jr., Psychology; Dr. Eugene K. Wolf, Music; and Dr. Sally H. Zigmond, Biology. We are particularly grateful to Dr. Allen, who generously shared materials on deciding where to apply.

In addition, we owe a particular debt to those who read and commented upon the revised version of this book: Dr. Peter Conn, English; Dr. Gregory Farrington, Engineering; Dr. Terry H. Fortune, Physics; and Dr. Ross A. Webber, Management.

Several individuals at other institutions generously agreed to review the original handbook when we were deciding whether to rewrite it for a broader audience: Dr. Reed Browning, Kenyon College; Mr. James Cogswell, University of Minnesota; Dr. Harry Evans, Fordham University; Dr. April Hamel, Washington University; Ms. Susan Kallenbach, New York University; Ms. Artemis Kirk, Simmons College; Dr. Joseph Mahoney, University of Illinois; Dr. Jack Nelson, Temple University; Ms. Joan O'Keefe, Brown University; Dr. Bruce Pollack-Johnson, Oberlin College; Dr. Leah Smith, Swarthmore College; and Dr. Robert Wood, Rutgers University, Camden. The anonymous reviewers for the University of Pennsylvania Press made several very helpful suggestions, from which the text has benefitted.

For years faculty members have generously shared their insight and experience at programs we have organized for graduate students. It is impossible to thank them all here individually, but we are well aware that, but for them, this book could not exist. We would, however, specifically like to acknowledge Dr. Herman Beavers for his thoughts on beginning a new faculty position. Graduate students, postdoctoral fellows, and junior faculty members have discussed their own job searches with us; they have broadened our awareness of the range of what may happen and increased our ability to predict what is likely to happen.

We are particularly grateful to those graduate students and alumni of the University of Pennsylvania who shared their sample job-hunting materials with us. Because we promised them anonymity, we cannot thank them here by name. However, their generosity has provided what many will find to be the most useful part of this book.

Our colleagues at the Career Planning and Placement Service at the University of Pennsylvania have been consistently encouraging and tolerant of the disruption writing a book imposes on a busy student-services office. We feel fortunate that its Director, Patricia Rose, has been unfailingly enthusiastic about and supportive of this project. Deborah Aukee, our systems specialist, made it much easier to produce a complex document. Deborah Gould was a sensitive, skilled, and patient indexer. Our assistants, Carol Waite and Debra Smiley, managed numerous details, and Patricia Bochi was a meticulous proofreader.

We want to thank Rich and Sara Heiberger and Jim, Emily, John, and David Vick for their interest in and support of this project.

Patricia Smith, Acquisitions Editor at the University of Pennsylvania Press, suggested we publish this book. We learned a great deal from her and particularly want to thank her.

Introduction

The Academic Job Search Handbook is designed to be a comprehensive guide to what is often a needlessly bewildering process. It is written to help new Ph.D.'s, as well as junior faculty members who are changing positions, benefit from the experience of those who have successfully survived the market. After years of working with doctoral students and speaking with faculty across disciplines about all aspects of the academic job search, we have found there are fundamental similarities in effective searches, whether one is a scientist, a social scientist, or a humanist. This book discusses the aspects of the search which must be managed by Ph.D.'s in both the arts and sciences and the professional disciplines.

The book begins with an overview of academic careers and institutional structures. It then takes you step-by-step through the application process, from establishing relationships with advisors years before going on the market, to making the most of a new position. Steps discussed include positioning yourself in the market, learning about job listings, preparing vitas, cover letters, and abstracts, discussing plans with those who will recommend you, participating in conferences, and negotiating offers. Sample vitas and cover letters, a timetable for your search, and an appendix of scholarly and professional associations are included.

Even if you are particularly interested in a few specific topics, we suggest that you read the book in its entirety. If you do, you will begin to see how advice on one topic is related to advice on another. If you understand the logic of the approach suggested in the situations we do discuss, you will be able to improvise effectively when you encounter a new situation.

Each discipline also has its own customs. What is "right" is frequently what is done in one's own field. Thus this guide should never replace the specific conventions of your discipline. You may find useful advice on job hunting from your national professional association. Faculty members in your own department will always be able to give the best perspective on your search. In job hunting, as in anything else, unanimity is rare. When expert advice conflicts, we hope that the handbook will have given you a perspective on which to base your own judgment.

The first version of this handbook was written for graduate students at the University of Pennsylvania, in consultation with the Graduate Faculty Placement Council, an advisory group to the University's Career Planning and Placement Service. As our students reported to us that they found it helpful, they also started sharing it with friends at other institutions, who began to request copies from us, as did some faculty members at other institutions. The present version is an extension of the original document, reviewed by an expanded group representing professional schools as well as arts and sciences departments.

We hope that the volume is helpful. Academic careers offer the opportunity for intensely satisfying and productive work. We hope that by clarifying some of the processes by which positions are obtained, we can reduce some of the anxiety and uncertainty of the job-hunting process so that candidates can get on with their chosen teaching and research.

Part I
What You Should Know
Before You Start

Chapter 1
The Structure of Academic Careers

You will be entering the job market at a time when higher education is subject to much self-scrutiny and external assessment. One of the safest statements that can be made about your academic career, which may well extend over the next forty to fifty years, is that it will probably be somewhat unlike those of your predecessors. Nevertheless, you are entering the market as it exists now, so it is important to understand how academic jobs have traditionally been organized.

The system of higher education in the United States is bewildering in its variety and complexity. Unlike many countries in the world, the United States has no national, in the sense of federally funded, universities. Its major universities, both private and state-funded, house faculties of arts and sciences and major professional schools. There are also small publicly funded institutions, and that peculiarly American institution, the four-year college, which is usually, but not always, private. Privately funded institutions are frequently secular, but are sometimes funded by religious institutions, whose religious influence on campus varies from nonexistent to omnipresent. Two-year community colleges constitute an increasingly important segment of higher education, but are mainly outside the scope of this book.

Both colleges and universities (or campuses of major universities) may enjoy either regional or national reputations. As a general rule, universities of national reputation place the most emphasis upon research as a criterion of success for faculty members. Teaching is most likely to be emphasized at less prestigious universities and at four-year colleges, although four-year colleges of national reputation also require substantial research of their faculty members.

Both student and faculty life are affected by conditions of faculty employment. At some institutions, nearly all faculty are full-time. Others use many part-time instructors. Faculty and other staff members at some institutions are unionized. Where unions exist, membership may be high across the board, or it may vary widely from school to school and department to department.

Career Ladders

Given the variety of institutions, the similarity of their promotional structures is surprisingly similar. The structure of academic hiring has been dominated by the tenure system, with a fairly orderly ladder that at most institutions leads from assistant professor, to associate professor (with tenure) to full professor. This "tenure track" route leads to status as a standing member of the faculty with full rights of participation in institutional decision making, and what is close to a lifetime guarantee of a job, barring economic upheaval or conviction for criminal activity.

Tenure-track positions have been supplanted in many institutions by a variety of positions conceived of as temporary: instructorships, lectureships, visiting and research assistant/associate professorships. They exist for a variety of reasons: to cover heavy teaching loads for introductory courses in a department that does not have enough, or any, graduate students to meet the demand; to replace a faculty member who is on sabbatical; to enable individuals able to secure research funds to be associated with a university.

Even though these positions may be held by the same individual and renewed over a period of several years, they are best thought of by job candidates as temporary, because they are outside the school's structure of permanent employment. In many cases holding such a position does not represent a "foot-in-the-door" for permanent employment with the department, because if a tenure-track position becomes available a national search will be conducted.

Hiring and promotion have tended to become less "genteel" and more market-driven in recent years, with no sign that the trend will be reversed. It has become less likely that candidates will obtain positions through a few phone calls made to an advisor, more likely that jobs will be nationally advertised, and more likely that institutions will compete for candidates using salaries, reduced teaching loads, and special research facilities.

Paths to Academic Administration

Educational institutions, even small ones, are also complex organizations that must be managed. They have physical plants, staff, investments, and budgets in at least the millions of dollars. Therefore they need the same sorts of managers as are found in the business world. Many of these individuals do not have academic backgrounds.

The management of academic programs, on the other hand, is a responsibility usually held by those who have followed an academic career path. Someone who is interested in academic administration typically begins by taking on a greater than ordinary share of administrative and committee tasks within his or her department and institution. A frequent path might lead from department chair, to dean, to provost, usually the chief academic officer. Some institutions choose their president from those who have followed this route. Others do not, looking for a president with substantial experience in a profession, business, or government, or on the business side of managing a university.

The climb to academic administration generally begins after at least obtaining tenure, and, more likely, as a full professor. Individuals who are strongly drawn to administrative activity can certainly find entry-level positions with good possibilities for promotion. It is likely, however, that they will have a lower ceiling on career advancement than those who have begun as faculty members.

Movement Between Institutions During a Career

Despite tenure's presumption of lifetime employment, faculty members do increasingly move between institutions in the course of a career. Typical occasions of moves may include not getting tenure at one institution; being "lured away" by another that is trying to build its department, at a higher salary or rank; responding to a job opportunity for a spouse or partner.

To some extent, there is a national hierarchy of colleges and universities, roughly correlated with the research reputations of their faculty members and their selectivity in admitting students. In addition, there is something of a national hierarchy of departments, based on approximately the same standards. For example, an institution of generally average quality may sometimes house one of the premier departments in a given discipline.

It is generally easier to move from an institution of higher status to one of lower status than in the other direction. To some extent, this is a function of "name recognition." In addition, the most prominent institutions generally provide the best facilities for research on the part of their faculty members, both in terms of equipment and libraries, and in reduced teaching loads. People at these institutions generally have more opportunities for the kind of research that will lead to additional opportunities. Therefore, candidates usually aim as high as possible in the choice of a first academic position.

Does this mean that a candidate who does not begin an academic career at a major research institution may never have a chance to be on the faculty of one? Of course not. Particularly in the tight job market of recent years, candidates have taken the best positions they were offered, continued to do research, and moved to other institutions within a few years. They have been able to make these moves through visibility generated from research, publication, and participation in national professional or scholarly organizations. It is the case, however, that if an individual does not move to an institution or department of national reputation within the first few years of a career, he or she becomes increasingly less likely to do so.

Some movement is also possible between academic and nonacademic institutions. This is particularly likely to be the case in professional schools, in which candidates may join the faculty at a senior level after achieving a distinguished record of accomplishment in the profession. Scientific and technical areas have also seen increasing movement between academic and industrial research settings.

However, transferability of credentials between academic and nonacademic settings varies greatly from field to field. It is a good idea to seek advice from senior individuals on both "sides" so that you do not make a major career move without being aware of its probable implications. You may need, for example, to learn how long scholars in your field can refrain from pursuing active research before they risk being unable to resume it with any credibility.

Chapter 2
Hiring from the Institution's Point of View

Just as your vita presents the public face of your qualifications in a simple, organized form, without revealing the full complexity of your individual life, an advertised position is the public presentation of an outcome of complex negotiations within a department and possibly within an institution.

It will generally be impossible for you, as a job candidate, to have a full understanding of what goes on behind the scenes. Even if you are fortunate enough to have an inside contact who can give you additional perspective, it is still extremely unlikely that you will know everything about the hiring decision. Thus, throughout the job search process, you will need to present yourself in the strongest fashion possible without tying yourself into knots trying to "second guess" the institution that has advertised the position.

However, here are some of the considerations that might be at work.

Defining and Advertising a Position

It may be fairly easy for a department to obtain approval and funding for a renewable lectureship or sabbatical replacement position. When a tenure-track position is listed, however, it reflects efforts by a department to maintain or strengthen its hiring position vis-à-vis other departments in the school. In today's financially stringent climate, approval to fill a position that has been vacated is not necessarily granted routinely. The department that has lost a staff member must defend to its dean the necessity of replacing the position. Meanwhile other departments are lobbying to expand their staff. If the hiring department has been given a new position, that very fact reflects even more intense departmental lobbying.

The definition of the position more frequently reflects discussion internal to the department. In some cases the definition is obvious: the department absolutely must replace a faculty member with a particular expertise. Perhaps, too, the department has a long-range plan that calls for increasing areas of strength in some orderly fashion. At other times, there may be dissension within the department about how the new position should be defined. Some want the department to move in one direction, some in another. The debate is resolved to the point necessary to define and advertise a position, but it does not necessarily mean that everyone has been convinced.

Further complicating the situation is the tendency of departments in recent years to advertise positions simultaneously at the assistant and associate professor levels, leaving the area of specialization entirely open. In that case, the department has clearly chosen to "see who's out there," planning to make an offer to whomever in its view is the best candidate. New Ph.D.'s are often unnecessarily frightened by an ad that mentions positions at both levels. The hiring department will not compare a new Ph.D. to a senior faculty member. The new Ph.D. will be compared to other new Ph.D.'s, the senior faculty member to other senior faculty members, and an offer will be made to the individual who both is the best candidate relative to his or her peer group and can best fit the needs of the department.

Implications for Candidates

A department that has gone to considerable trouble to get funding for a position will not take kindly to applicants who seem to view it as a second-best alternative to be abandoned as soon as something better comes along. Therefore, it is important that you as a candidate convey a serious interest in the position throughout the search process. Don't get bogged down in self-comparisons to imagined other candidates. Concentrate on communicating what you have to offer. It may be even more appropriate and desirable than you realize.

Screening Candidates

All faculty members in a small department may be involved in hiring, whereas in a larger one the logistics of managing the search, and a good deal of decision making, may be delegated to a search committee. In some cases the committee may include a student representative. In most hiring bodies, there will be some members of the group who are intensely interested in who is ultimately hired and who take the process very seriously; others who take participation seriously, but view it as an obligation that interferes with things they would rather be doing; and, possibly, an individual who wishes he or she were elsewhere and who participates without giving the process full attention.

The hiring group will read through the materials submitted in response to the advertisement. In some cases, the first goal will be to identify a smaller group, who will be asked to provide additional materials such as dissertation chapters or articles. In other cases, those who are to be interviewed at a convention or who are to be directly invited to campus for an interview will be chosen from the materials sent initially.

At this stage candidates, of necessity, get the least careful screening, because it simply is not possible to do an in-depth evaluation of what may be up to several hundred sets of materials sent in response to an advertisement. Individuals in the hiring group are probably not yet wedded to the candidates they prefer, because most of these are still abstractions, presented on paper.

Therefore, if someone asks the group to pay special attention to a candidate at this stage, the request is likely to be honored. The request may take the form of a phone call from a dean who says, "X is the spouse of Y, who is department Z's top choice. We'll lose her unless we can make an offer to him. See what you think." It may take the form of a phone call from a department member's former dissertation advisor who says, "Dr. L. is the best student the department has had in the last five years and she is seriously interested in this job. Can you be sure to look at her application carefully?"

Implications for Candidates

As will be discussed in detail in later chapters, make all the materials used in your application clear and accessible, even to someone who is not a specialist in your area. Don't be afraid to be slightly redundant. For example, if your cover letter repeats some of the material in your vita, someone who does not pay full attention to one may pick up key points from the other.

Consider asking a senior faculty member from your Ph.D.-granting institution whether he or she knows anyone at the school to which you are applying, and then ask for a phone call on your behalf. This call can draw attention to your candidacy and help keep your vita in the group of those chosen for further examination.

Interviewing

In some fields, departments interview many candidates at a national convention and then invite a smaller group for second interviews on campus. In other fields, the campus interview is the first and only one.

Once the interviewing process begins, issues of personality, style, and the department's own history begin to come into play, in unpredictable fashion. Most departments have their own histories of hiring "successes" and "mistakes." Naturally they will attempt to repeat one and avoid the other. Therefore, statements made by a candidate during an interview may have resonances unknown to the candidate. For example, if your remarks closely parallel those of a candidate hired two years ago, they will probably be heard differently depending on the current consensus as to whether hiring that candidate was a coup or a mistake.

As a candidate, you are unlikely to have a full understanding of power and influence within the department. Obviously, you must be chosen by the hiring committee and approved by the chairperson. In addition, however, there may exist individuals of sufficient influence that the department may be reluctant to hire anyone to whom they strongly object.

Implications for Candidates

Before going to an interview, get all the first-hand information about a department that you can possibly gather. However, you should recognize that you are unlikely, at best, to gain more than a partial understanding of the departmental dynamics. Therefore, don't try to second guess your interviewers. Again, concentrate on the clear communication of what you have to say.

Decision Making

After a small number of candidates have been invited to campus for an interview, the department must decide to whom to offer the position. Sometimes the choice is simple; sometimes it is agonizing. Faced with the real people who have interviewed for the position, rather than the "ideal" represented by the ad, the department may need to make very concrete trade-offs. What if the candidate who is ideal in terms of the qualities described in the ad has charmed one-half of the department and totally alienated the other? What if no one really fits the job that was envisioned, but one candidate seems outstanding in every other respect?

The department must make its decisions knowing that job offers and acceptances are occurring over the space of a few months. It knows the largest salary that it can pay, and it knows that it must give its first-choice candidate at least a week or two to decide whether to accept the offer. It may believe that the first-choice candidate is extremely unlikely to accept the position, and that the second-choice candidate, also very good, is likely to accept, but only if it is offered within the next few weeks. Finally, if none of the candidates seems entirely satisfactory, the department must decide whether to leave the position vacant for a year and risk losing it to some kind of budgetary constraint.

Usually the department comes to a decision that balances competing priorities. Depending upon the department's style, a job may be offered to the candidate who has not alienated anyone, to the candidate who is most strongly backed by a few influential department members, to the candidate who appears most neutral in terms of some controversy that has split the department, or to a candidate chosen in some other fashion.

Implications for Candidates

Do your best to accept the fact that hiring is not usually a matter of choosing the "best" candidate by some set of abstract criteria, but of making a reasonable choice among valid, if competing, priorities, an inherently political process. Do your best, therefore, not to dismiss the process as somehow unethical. If each member of a hiring committee honestly thinks a different candidate is the best choice for the department, a decision must be made somehow. Unless it is to be settled by a duel or a flip of a coin, it must be decided through a negotiated process that acknowledges several factors not necessarily known to the candidates.

If you insist on thinking either that there is an obviously "best" candidate for every job and that every time that person has not been chosen an immoral decision has been made, or that hiring is a random process amounting to no more than the luck of the draw, you will diminish your own ability to understand the difference between what is and is not in your control. Worse, you risk becoming angry, bitter, or cynical, and, therefore, approaching potential employers with a visible presumption that they will be unfair.

Approach a department as if you expect it to behave in a fair and reasonable fashion. Make it easy for those who would like to hire you to lobby for you, by being well-prepared and by communicating an attitude of respect for everyone you meet during the course of a day. Let your enthusiasm for the position be obvious.

Keep a record of the people with whom you speak during each application. Even if you do go elsewhere, you can keep in touch with them, send papers to them, and cultivate them over the years. They may invite you back after you establish a reputation elsewhere.

Negotiation and Acceptance

Once a position is offered, there may be a brief period of negotiation about salary, terms of employment (for example, research facilities, or how many classes are to be taught in the first year), and time given the candidate to make a decision. Sometimes there will be delays, as the department must receive approval from a higher level before making a specific offer. Usually other finalists will be notified of a decision only after a candidate has definitely accepted a position.

Implications for Candidates

Understand that delays may be inevitable. However, if your own situation changes (for example, if you get another offer), do not hesitate to let the department know. If you are turned down, you may wish to ask for constructive feedback. This is acceptable, and frequently useful, but bear in mind that the person to whom you are speaking may not be able to be entirely open with you about how a decision was made. Concentrate your questions on what you might have done to strengthen your presentation, rather than on how the decision was made.

Was the Job Wired?

Sometimes, at the conclusion of a search, it is widely perceived that the advertised position was not truly open. There was a high probability at the outset that an offer would be made to someone who was already within the department; to someone whom the department had been wooing for the last few years; to a member of a group whose underrepresentation among faculty members was viewed as an intolerable situation; to a clone of those already in the department; and so on.

Implications for Candidates

Compete for every job you want as if you have a genuine chance of being offered it, whatever you guess or have been told. That way you best position yourself to take advantage of the uncertainty inherent in every hiring situation. Maybe the department did have a strong front-runner, but he or she will not accept the position in the end. Maybe you are very unlikely to get this job, but the campus interview you are offered will help you polish your interviewing skills so that you will do better at the next interview.

Remember that, even if you are not successful in getting a particular job, you have left behind an impression of abilities, talents, and personality. Frequently, faculty members will talk with other faculty members at other schools about good candidates whom they interviewed but were not able to hire. Even if your interview at a particular school is unsuccessful, it can serve as good advertising, depending upon how you deal with the interview situation and, particularly, with any rejection.

When you are hired, there may well be disappointed candidates who think that you had some kind of unfair advantage, so try to be generous in your assessment of the decisions made by what are, by and large, well-intentioned people.

Part II
Planning and Timing
Your Search

Chapter 3
Becoming a Job Candidate: The Timetable for Your Search

It is important to begin to prepare for your job search well before you finish your dissertation; it is also important to time the search to coincide with the definite completion of your dissertation. In your last two years of doctoral study, think about your job search, your participation in scholarly organizations, and the completion of your dissertation as a unified whole. Most faculty members will advise you not to take a tenure-track position before your dissertation is completed. A strong logic informs that view. Once you have accepted a position, you will gain tenure as a result of research done as a junior faculty member. If you begin your research by completing the dissertation, you will already be late by the "tenure-clock," and in the position of a student with several incompletes, who can never catch up with current work.

Funding considerations may force you to look for paid employment before your dissertation is completed. If this is the case, discuss the situation with faculty members in your department, and choose the employment most conducive to finishing the dissertation. You will be in the strongest position to obtain a good tenure-track position in the year in which your dissertation is definitely completed, or, in some cases, in the year after that.

Use the timetable below to plan your job search while completing your dissertation and participating in scholarly activities. Each suggested step is discussed in detail elsewhere in this book. If, by chance, you read it thinking, "I wish I had done some of these things last year," don't despair! Fill in the gaps as best you can. Certainly many people obtain positions without having conducted the "perfect" job search. However, if you see gaps in your preparation and do not do as well as you hope in the job market this year, you may find much more success if you go on the market again next year after better preparation.

Timetable for Applying for Jobs That Begin in September

Two Years Before

- Make sure all members of your dissertation committee are selected. Consider getting a December degree which enables you to apply with "degree in hand." (Foreign nationals, however, should consider the visa implications of this timing.) Learn about conference dates and locations. Plan to attend, and, if feasible, to give a presentation. Learn deadlines for submitting papers.
- Learn about all the important sources of job listings in your field. In some disciplines the job listings of one scholarly association cover almost everything. In other fields there may be multiple sources.
- Give thought to your long-range goals and consider the kinds of jobs you will wish to apply for. If your plans will have an impact on a spouse or partner, begin to talk with that person about geographic locations you will both consider acceptable.

Summer, Fifteen Months Before

- Make sure your dissertation will be finished no later than the summer before the job begins, and preferably earlier. In some fields many institutions will not consider a candidate without a Ph.D. in hand.
- Discuss your plans with your advisor and any others in the department who may be interested. If they don't think you will be ready to go on the market until the following year, consider their point of view very seriously. If you begin a new position and have not yet completed your dissertation, you will start off behind schedule in terms of the "tenure clock."
- Renew contacts with faculty members whom you may know at other institutions, letting them know of your progress and that you will be on the market soon.
- If you haven't already done so, set up a credentials file at your campus career center. Get letters of recommendation from those with whom you will have no further significant contact.
- Prepare your vita.
- Consider giving a paper at a major conference in your field or submitting an article or articles to major journals in your field. Find out deadlines for calls for papers.

Fall, Twelve Months Before

- Finalize your vita. (You may need to update it a few times during the year.)
- Arrange for letters of recommendation to be written by everyone who will support your search. Your advisor will probably update his or her letter as your dissertation passes through its final stages. Give copies of your transcript, vita, and a chapter of your dissertation to those writing for you.
- Be prepared to provide an employer with a copy of the first chapter of your dissertation, a research paper, your vita, and a copy of your transcript.
- Keep working on your dissertation!
- Attend any campus programs that may be offered on academic interviewing.
- Watch carefully for job listings and apply for everything that interests you. If you notice that advertisements request other written materials (e.g., dissertation abstract, statement of research interest), take time now to prepare excellent ones. The first cover letters you write may take longer to compose than subsequent ones.
- Continue to keep in close touch with your advisor.
- Consider making a few direct inquiries at departments that particularly interest you (what you are most likely to discover in this way are non-tenure track positions), if you can define reasonable criteria for selecting the departments.
- Review the literature in your field and subfield in preparation for interviews.
- Check to see that letters of application have been received by the departments to which you apply.

Eight Months Before

- Interviewers will ask you about your long-range research plans. Even if you are so immersed in your dissertation that you can't see beyond it at the moment, take time to give some thought to where your research will lead.
- Many conferences are held now. It is important to attend them and take advantage of the opportunity they provide for the formal and informal exchange of information.
- Prepare carefully for each interview. If you give a presentation as

part of an interview day on campus, practice it in advance. Remember to send thank-you notes after each interview.

- Continue to look, apply, and interview for positions.
- This may well be a stressful time. Plan to take some breaks for activities or events that you consider relaxing and renewing.

Six Months Before

- Continue to apply for and interview for positions, although most openings will have been announced by now.
- You may begin to get offers. If you feel you need more time to make a decision about an offer, don't hesitate to ask for it. You will, however, have to abide by whatever time frame you and the employer agree on for your decision. You don't need to be totally open with everyone at this stage, but you must be completely honest. When you do accept a position, consider your acceptance a binding commitment.
- If the offers you want are not coming in, don't think that you must take absolutely any job that is offered to you, whether you want it or not. The job market will come around again next year. Talk with your advisor and others about the best way to position yourself for next year's market, if necessary. You can also keep watching for one-year appointments, which are often announced later than tenure-track positions.
- After you have accepted a job, take time to thank everyone who has been helpful to you in the process.

Chapter 4
Deciding Where and When to Apply

Before you begin a job search, it is necessary to think about what kind of job you want. Think about the following questions as you prepare to enter the job market. Although some are most applicable in fields in which there is high demand, the issues they raise are important even in tight job markets. Your thoughts about these questions can help you to communicate with your advisor and others who will assist you in your job search, to prepare for interviewing, and to assess job offers.

Understanding the Market

You must know something about the job market before you begin your search. The more informed you are the better your search will be. The experience of graduate students a few years ahead of you in your department provides a very limited knowledge base. You need to be conversant with the following:

- What is the hiring outlook in your discipline?
- What is the hiring outlook in your field of research?
- How broad is the market in your field? Opportunities may exist outside traditional departmental definitions. For example, although your degree is from an arts and sciences department, might you seek a position in a professional school (such as business, government, communications)? Would a short-term experience, such as a postdoctoral appointment, increase your long-term options?
- How great is the competition for positions in your field at prestigious institutions? What is realistically required should you choose to compete for them? For example, would several publications be required?
- If you are in a highly specialized field, when and where are openings anticipated?

There are several ways you can obtain this information. Do a search on ERIC, an education database available in most university libraries, to find articles and reports about the job market in general and your discipline in particular. Read articles in *The Chronicle of Higher Education*. Contact your scholarly association (see Appendix 1) for reports it may have produced about the market. Check to see whether your campus career planning and placement office or graduate dean's office has records of the jobs taken by new Ph.D.'s from your school. Talk with students in your department who are on the market or recent graduates who have new faculty positions. Above all, talk regularly with your department chair, advisor, and other faculty members about the job market in your field.

Deciding Where to Apply

Institutional Characteristics

Are you willing or eager to consider jobs at:

- Public or private institutions?
- Large universities or small four-year teaching colleges or community colleges?
- A school with a distinctive institutional personality, such as a women's college, an institution with a strong religious affiliation, or a school offering an "innovative curriculum"?
- An institution that emphasizes research over teaching or one that emphasizes teaching over research?
- A place that demands or offers heavy involvement in the life of the school (usually a teaching college) or one in which your major identification will be with your department?
- A highly selective institution or one that prides itself on offering educational opportunities to a broad section of the community?
- An institution where the faculty is unionized or one where individual salaries are market-driven?
- An institution that compensates new faculty members with salary or one that compensates them with prestige?

Departmental Characteristics

Do you prefer:

- Many colleagues in your field of research or an opportunity to be the in-house expert in your field?
- Opportunity to and expectation that you will socialize with others in

the department or an atmosphere that encourages solely professional involvement?

- An emphasis on graduate or on undergraduate teaching?
- A department in which you would be the first person of your social background ever hired, or one in which you feel most people are like you?
- A department with a specific orientation ("traditional," "radical," "applied") or one whose faculty members take a variety of approaches?
- A department where teaching occurs mainly in seminars or one where classes are primarily large lectures?
- A department that emphasizes research or one that emphasizes teaching?
- A department with a hierarchical structure or one that emphasizes participatory decision making?

Geographic Considerations

- Do you have any geographic restrictions or preferences?
- Is it important to you to be in a rural, small city, suburban or urban environment?
- Does your research require resources that are available in limited geographic locations?
- Can you work and live comfortably in any region of the country?
- Will you need to limit the geographic range of your search because of personal considerations, such as the career plans of a partner, a child's education, or the need to be near a relative who is ill?
- Will you look only in the United States or will you expand your search to other countries? Are you able to teach in a language other than English?

Additional Personal Considerations

Additional idiosyncratic personal considerations may be important in your job search. Even if you are the only candidate in the world who will choose one position over another because it will give you the most opportunity and time to use your pilot's license, take this preference into consideration if it is important to you.

How Competitive Are You?

Be realistic in evaluating the type of institution where you will be able and willing to do what is necessary to attain tenure.

- In some fields, it is very important to be able to obtain funding for your own research. Do you feel willing and able to do this?
- Are you able to resist pressure from your own departmental culture to apply only to certain kinds of institutions?
- What balance do you want to strike between career-related features and non-professional aspects of a job? For example, would you take a position at a highly prestigious institution at which you would need to work nearly all your waking hours in order to have a reasonable chance of obtaining tenure?
- Do you see a discrepancy between your ability and willingness to perform in your first job and your ability to obtain it? For example, are you highly productive in research and publication and very awkward in oral presentations and conversations? In that case, work to improve your job-hunting skills instead of letting them limit your job search, because your job-hunting ability can always improve if you are willing to give it practice and attention. On the other hand, if you interview extremely well but seriously doubt your ability or willingness to perform outstanding research, don't talk yourself into a job whose demands you may not want or be able to meet.

When to Look

Because most jobs are advertised about a year before they are to begin, you will probably start your job search while you are still finishing your dissertation. It is crucial that you discuss with your advisor when to begin the search, because he or she will be knowledgeable about the advisability of being a candidate with an unfinished dissertation as opposed to one with the degree in hand. That is the most important factor in determining when to start looking.

On the other hand, if you are in a field with very few annual openings, and a good job is announced before you are entirely ready to apply, you and your advisor may decide that it is a good idea for you to accelerate your search. If it looks as if you will finish in a year in which very few openings are available, plan to search for good interim opportunities while you conduct the academic job search. Many postdoctoral and other fellowship opportunities, like academic positions, have very early deadlines for application.

If you are an international student, you should find out if there are visa considerations that might affect the timing of your search and the date when you might prefer to have your degree awarded. Start working on this task early to avoid problems or delays that might prevent an institution from offering you a job later on, or that might compromise your ability to remain long-term in the United States if that is your desire. If your campus has an office that offers good visa and immigration advising, use it. If not, consult a reputable immigration attorney.

Discussing Your Plans with Others

Sharing your thoughts with your advisor, department placement chair, and others who will work with you in your search can help these individuals act effectively on your behalf. Conversation with them can help you clarify your own thinking as it evolves. Honest faculty feedback about how realistic your choices are can be enormously helpful to you. The best way for you to elicit it is to ask for candor, assuring those you ask that your feelings will not be hurt by what you hear. Needless to say, respond in a way that does not cause someone to regret his or her candor.

In talking to others, whether faculty members or peers, keep your own priorities clearly in mind, and use your own judgment. Consider, for instance, your feelings about raising research funds. In some fields, such as the sciences and engineering, you must do so successfully and repeatedly to achieve tenure at a major research institution. If you have a realistic chance of obtaining a position at a major research institution, but privately feel that meeting the research demands necessary to get tenure there will consign you to years of prolonged misery, then it may be wise for you to look at another type of institution.

Perhaps your graduate work has only recently begun to take off because you were meeting personal obligations that you are now convinced will be lighter. In that case you may want to try for jobs that your advisor feels are beyond your reach, even if you need to take a postdoctoral position in the interim to strengthen your credentials. If you are a natural risk-taker convinced that a small but growing department may be the source of some of the most exciting work in your field, you may choose to ignore the cautions of more conservative friends who say, "Yes, but who's ever heard of it?"

Following your own instincts as to what you will find satisfying is easy if your goals are similar to those of the people around you. It is often more difficult if you want to follow a path that seems foreign to your advisor and most of the students in your department. In that case, use their skepticism as a prod to make sure that you get as much information as possible so that you make informed decisions. If you want to do something non-traditional, be able to explain your decision to others so they can support your search.

Balance this skepticism, however, with the enthusiasm of people who are doing what you would like to do, even if they are at other institutions and you have to seek them out. In the end, it is your career and your life, and you are most likely to be satisfied with both if you shape them according to your own priorities and values.

Chapter 5
The Importance of Advisors and Professional Networks

A job search may feel like a lonely enterprise, but it is always conducted within the context of a web of social relationships. You work within a discipline with its own language, conventions, and structure of communication. Your own research has undoubtedly been strengthened by communication with other people; in some fields it has been conducted as part of a team. You are leaving a department with one social structure and culture to enter another. You will be explicitly recommended by several people, and those who are considering your candidacy may hear about you from others.

Whether you find these facts reassuring or alarming, by taking account of them as early as possible in your graduate career, you can brighten your prospects in the job market. If you have not paid sufficient attention to them until now, it is not too late to focus on them.

Advisors and Mentors

It is difficult to overemphasize the importance of an advisor in an academic career. When you enter the job market, and perhaps for years, you will often to be viewed as "X's student." If your advisor is well known in the market you want to enter, thinks highly of you, spends time with you, is savvy about the employment market, and is enthusiastically supportive of your job search, you will be likely to think highly of the importance of the advisor's role. Your first job search may well go more smoothly, because you will be able to discuss your goals with your advisor, who will in turn perhaps make phone calls that will pave the way to interviews.

While such a situation is generally enviable, you may also need to make a particular effort to distinguish between your own goals and your advisor's goals for you, if you feel they differ. Making choices that are disappointing to the advisor will be particularly difficult. You also may rely too heavily on your advisor's intervention and fail to master job-hunting skills as thoroughly as does someone who gets less assistance. If you are blessed with such an advisor, make a particular effort to learn from that person how best to make efforts on your own behalf.

You may have a less-than-ideal advising relationship. Perhaps your advisor is not particularly well known, brilliant but unskilled at interacting with other people, so formal and distant that you are honestly unsure what he or she thinks about your work, or, in fact, disappointed in your work and not hesitant to tell you so. Whatever the characteristics of this real human being, you can probably improve the relationship, profit from the individual's greatest strengths, and, if necessary, find additional mentors.

If things are not going well between you and your advisor, your natural tendency may be to avoid talking with him or her. Resist this temptation! It is only through interaction that you can identify problems and attempt to address them. Arrange regular meetings to discuss your work, come well prepared for them, ask for as much feedback as you can get, take your advisor's suggestions, and make sure he or she sees that you have done so. If you sense that your advisor is not happy with what you are doing but is not telling you why, ask more directly for feedback. You may learn that in fact there is no problem, or you may identify an issue you can address.

Even though advisors have considerable power, it is not unlimited. Most will respect you more if you think independently, respectfully express disagreement when it exists, present your ideas persuasively, and generally act as if you accept responsibility for your own career.

Most advisors act responsibly; a few abuse their power. The latter are most likely to victimize those who are unwilling to challenge inappropriate treatment. If you honestly believe you are being treated unfairly or inappropriately, begin by learning what the norms for acceptable behavior are. For example, your advisor may be crediting your work appropriately according to standards in your field while you may feel it is being "stolen." You can ask questions of other faculty members and graduate students, see whether your institution has formal policies and guidelines governing the relationship between advisors and students, consult publications of your professional association, and use library resources to understand how your experience fits into the general scheme of things.

Whatever your relationship with your advisor, it is helpful to have as many senior people as possible interested in your success. Take advantage of every opportunity to talk to and get to know other faculty members in your department. Ask them for opinions, perspective, and feedback in areas where you genuinely value their expertise. It is not necessary or desirable to think of this interaction in terms of flattery. Research enterprises flourish on the exchange of ideas.

Your peers in the department offer another valuable source of perspective and lifelong contacts. Be realistic about the extent to which you will be competing with them in the job market; many candidates overestimate it. By and large, you have different strengths and interests. You will be far more successful if you exchange information and ideas with other students than if you avoid interaction for fear of somehow giving them a competitive edge. Beware, however, of becoming too involved in exchanging job-hunt horror stories. Every department has its share; some are apocryphal, and overindulgence in listening to and recounting them blurs your perspective.

Professional Associations

Ideally, even in the early years of graduate study, you have begun to develop membership in professional networks that extend beyond your department and university. Whatever your field, there is at least one, if not several, scholarly or professional associations devoted to the exchange of ideas. Conferences, publications, and local and regional meetings are the most common means of exchange. Because of the importance of these organizations, they will be referred to again and again throughout this handbook. If you don't know those that are important in your field, ask faculty members in your department.

Calls for papers are probably posted in your department. You can also consult the "Deadlines" section of *The Chronicle of Higher Education* for such notices. If you feel that publications in major journals or presentations at national conventions are slightly beyond your reach at this point, look for regional or local meetings of national organizations and respectable but less prestigious journals. Attend as many presentations as you can. In addition to learning and gaining ideas from the material presented, you can see how others present their work, and form your own conclusions about the most effective way to communicate ideas.

Individual Communication

If you are interested in the work of someone at another institution, whether you learn of it through a conference, a publication, or word of mouth, it is appropriate to approach that person, by phone, mail, or E-mail, for a further exchange of ideas. Share your comments; send a copy of a related paper or a reprint of an article you wrote. Ask questions. Suggest a meeting at a conference you both will be attending. It goes without saying that your comments and questions should be sincere and intelligent. Given that, however, by taking the initiative you greatly expand the range of intellectual resources upon which you can draw and develop a broad network of professional contacts with whom you can remain in touch throughout your career.

As more and more researchers participate in worldwide electronic networks, the range of possibilities for communication becomes even more vast. All you need to participate is a terminal, a modem, and access to a mainframe computer connected to such a network. You may well find a national or international network of individuals with similar professional concerns who share their ideas on a daily basis. Perhaps you already participate in a sophisticated network. If so, periodically check to make sure that you understand the scope of its resources. If you have not yet begun to exploit this technology, you can probably find information at the computer center on your campus. Reference librarians will probably be the campus gurus about on-line databases to which one can subscribe for a fee.

Observers of people's responses to electronic communication have frequently noted that it tends to flow across normal hierarchical boundaries. If you find very senior individuals who actively contribute to electronic bulletin boards or who are avid users of electronic mail, you may find this a comfortable way to communicate with them.

You impoverish your own work if you do not take advantage of the multiplicity of forums for the exchange of ideas and of the personal give-and-take that turns a good piece of work into an excellent one. While you should not do so for this reason alone, as you establish your own network of communication, you also expand the range of people who are interested in your success in the job market.

Chapter 6
Conference Presentations and Networking

Conferences and conventions are a major means of scholarly communication. They also provide an opportunity to meet people who can hire you or refer you to others who can. By the time you are an advanced graduate student, if not before, you should begin to participate in these meetings, which are an important means of communication in your discipline. As you near the end of your graduate work and enter the job market, conferences begin to play a more formal role in your job search. They may offer a job placement service or give you an opportunity to gain favorable exposure through presenting a paper, and they always give you a way to network informally with others.

You should almost certainly plan to attend the national meeting of the major association in your field in the year you are on the job market. If you can arrange to give a paper or participate in a poster session, try to do so.

Presentations

Each field has its own style for the delivery of presentations. If you are delivering a conference paper for the first time, ask your department what to expect and how to be prepared for it. In addition, check with your professional association to see whether it provides guidelines that help you answer the following questions.

Mode of Delivery

- Do you sit or stand?
- Do you speak from notes or read a paper?
- Do you answer questions at a "poster session"?

- How formally are papers presented? Is any form of humor ever appropriate?
- How long will you have to speak?
- Will there be questions from the audience? Will there be a moderator?

Visual Aids

- Should you prepare handouts?
- Should you use overhead transparencies or slides?
- How large should a poster be?

Practice your presentation before you offer it. If you can give a departmental seminar, so much the better, but, in any case, deliver the talk to an audience that will give you feedback. If you will use visual aids, include them in your practice session so that you are thoroughly comfortable handling them. Ask your colleagues to question the vulnerable points in your thesis so that you can practice fielding them. As you practice, make sure to speak loudly enough to be heard; look at your audience; and speak rapidly enough to hold your audience's attention but slowly enough that they can understand you.

Your visual aids should look as professional as you can make them. Have plenty of white space so they are easy to read. Keep material away from the outer edges of transparencies so the audience can read them even if they slip out of place on the projector. Avoid using dark background colors on slides. They absorb the heat from the projector lamp and pop out of focus. Check to make sure that materials when projected are clear from a distance. Your campus almost certainly has individuals who are expert in graphic presentation. Seek them out and use their help.

Visual and oral presentations should reinforce each other. The point of both is to communicate clearly and well, while maintaining the interest of the audience. Neither the communication style, orally or on the screen, should ever get in the way of the information.

Networking

Conferences vary in size according to your field, but they always offer you an opportunity to meet more people in your discipline in one place than you can ever encounter elsewhere. Even if they are not hiring, they are a source of potential information about their institutions, their departments, and their research. They may share information or remember you when you later apply to their departments; they may be people you can later contact for information.

But how do you meet them? Here are some suggestions:

- Find out which faculty members from your department will attend. If there is anyone to whom you would particularly like to be introduced, see if they can help you.
- Find out whether your department will give a party at the conference. If it will, be sure to attend. If not, see whether you can interest the department in arranging one.
- Give a presentation or poster session.
- Wear your nametag, and don't be shy about introducing yourself. Don't assume people will remember you.
- Attend sessions that interest you and talk with the speakers afterward, using your interest in their presentations as an icebreaker.
- Participate in smaller interest groups which may have meetings apart from presentations. Some organizations, for example, have active women's groups.
- If possible, take part in informal social gatherings attended by members of your department and faculty from other institutions.
- Much information gets exchanged at receptions and informal social gatherings. If you are comfortable joining a group you don't know and introducing yourself, by all means do so.
- Arrange brief meetings with someone whose work particularly interests you in advance of the conference, independent of a hiring context. Most fields are fairly small worlds, and having people know you is helpful, even if not immediately so.
- If there is a choice of hotels, stay in whichever is the main site for the conference. The central location will justify any extra expense because it will make it easier to meet people.

It is appropriate to walk up even to well-established faculty or researchers and introduce yourself. Few people consider this an imposition. In fact, both established and less well-known faculty find it very flattering when a student introduces him- or herself and says, "I've looked forward to meeting you."

If you are shy, you may prefer to meet people in structured situations. If you are very outgoing, it may be easier to introduce yourself to strangers. In either case, remember that networking works only if you make a good impression! When you meet new people, your interest in their work, your work, and the field should dominate your conversation.

If you are seeking information, elicit it naturally in the course of conversation. If people feel that your main interest is to pump them for job information, you would be better off not speaking with them in the first place. Avoid being overly pushy with or fawning over established researchers. Courtesy and consideration are good guidelines. People who are considering a candidate for a faculty position are looking not only for someone who is creative and smart and has a great future, but also for someone who is going to be a good colleague, that is, pleasant to have around and work with.

A conference mixes social and professional events and behaviors. As a job candidate, keep the professional aspect of the gathering foremost in your mind. There is the possibility that someone you approach may assume that your interest is social or romantic rather than professional. This still is more likely to be a problem for women, but occasionally is problematic for men as well. Make sure that your manner and attire convey a professional interest. If you are in doubt whether this is clear to the other person, stick to public settings (meetings and restaurants rather than suites or rooms), don't drink too much yourself, and disengage yourself from anyone who has.

Participating in a professional network is a valuable activity that will help you, not only in your search for your first position, but throughout your career as well. From it come possibilities for collaborative efforts, invitations to submit papers, and professional stimulation. So it's worthwhile to begin the process, whether it comes easily or with difficulty.

Chapter 7
Letters of Recommendation

As you learn about job openings, you will want to be prepared to respond to them as quickly as possible. At some point in the screening process for nearly every job, and frequently as part of your initial application, you will be asked to ensure that letters supporting your candidacy reach the hiring department. The number requested varies, but three is typical. Because letters require the cooperation of others, allow yourself plenty of time to obtain them.

Choosing Your Recommenders and Asking for Letters

The choice of recommenders is important and merits careful thought. Your dissertation advisor, of course, and anyone else with whom you have worked closely will be your first and second letter writers. In choosing additional recommenders find someone who can talk about your teaching, as well as a senior person who is still very much an active researcher. Most of your letters will probably be from your own department, but it is also acceptable to ask for letters from scholars outside your institution, if they are very familiar with your work.

Of course it is helpful to have a letter from someone who is widely known in your field, but do not ask people to write on your behalf unless they really know your work. Faculty generally agree that letters from students you have taught are not convincing on their own. However, if you are applying to a school that emphasizes excellent teaching, one of your faculty recommenders may quote from student comments about your teaching. In some professional fields, such as business and architecture, a letter from a former employer or consulting client may be helpful, especially for a school that values interaction with practitioners.

Ask for letters as much in advance as possible. Faculty members receive many requests for them. Phrase your request in such a way that if someone does not feel comfortable writing for you, he or she can gracefully decline. A tactful approach might be, "I'd appreciate a recommendation from you if you feel you know my work well enough to recommend me." If there is someone who must serve as a recommender, such as an advisor, about whose opinion of your work you are in doubt, you may want to ask that person to discuss with you frankly the types of institutions for which he or she can enthusiastically support your candidacy.

Discuss your plans with those who agree to write for you. Recommendations are most effective when they describe you as well-suited to a particular goal. If appropriate, remind the person who will recommend you of your work and experience. Provide him or her with your vita, a copy of a paper you wrote, a dissertation chapter, a statement of your research goals, or anything else that would be helpful.

Phone Calls

Sometimes a search committee, seeking what they feel will be a more candid evaluation, will call one or more of your recommenders. This is particularly likely to be the case when the recommender is known to someone at the hiring institution. Since letters of recommendation are almost uniformly positive, a spontaneous enthusiastic response to a potential employer's phone call is very helpful to you.

On the other hand, if the person who is called is totally surprised that you are applying to the institution which is calling, it probably does not help your case. Thus, it is very important to keep recommenders apprised of every step of your job search. You can ask them to reassure those who call about any aspects of your candidacy that you believe schools may find problematic. For example, if you are married to someone who is genuinely willing to move to the location where you take a job, your recommender can reinforce your statement that this is true.

Avoiding Negative Evaluations

Unfortunately, sometimes the difficult situation arises in which someone who would normally be expected to be supportive of your job search, such as an advisor, is not. Perhaps he or she is disappointed by the goals you have set, or believes they are unrealistic. Perhaps he or she genuinely does not believe you are as strong as other advisees in the past and does not want to compromise a reputation by giving you a recommendation stronger than he or she believes you deserve. Perhaps the person is retaliating for your resistance to some form of harassment. Perhaps you are merely the victim of hostility generated in another area of the person's life.

Whatever the cause, this situation is always difficult. Most likely you hear of it from someone else who reports to you what has been said in a letter or conversation. Perhaps you feel (rightly or wrongly) that, where you might expect to find support, you are encountering an obstacle. Several approaches are available to you, none totally risk-free, but all, on balance, more likely to be productive than is suffering in silence.

Direct Conversation

If you are dealing with a reasonable person who honestly does not think highly of your abilities, at least in relation to the arena in which you have chosen to compete, direct conversation may be productive. For example, you might begin by saying, "I know that you think I'm overreaching in some of my applications. Could you give me examples of institutions for which you could honestly be supportive of my candidacy?" It is helpful for you to remind yourself that no one has an obligation to strongly recommend a candidate against his or her better judgment. Even if the person's assessment of you is incorrect, he or she does have the right to an opinion.

Advice

If you can find a knowledgeable person of whom to ask advice, it can be very helpful. In choosing someone in whom to confide, consider that person's judgment, experience, and willingness to keep your communication confidential. Individuals outside your department may be particularly helpful in the latter regard. Counselors in university counseling centers and career planning and placement offices have a professional obligation to keep conversations confidential. So do campus ombudsmen, affirmative action officers, and staff members of other organizations, such as women's centers, chartered to protect the interests of members of a particular group.

On the other hand, while such professionals may make a good sounding board, they are unlikely to know enough about the personalities of people in your department to be able to give you very specific advice. Another faculty member in the department is in the best position to suggest how you may strengthen your position with whoever is obstructing your search or, on occasion, to tactfully intervene. Also consider your dean's office. Frequently, the dean's office is structured so that an associate dean is responsible for graduate education. A good associate dean is a great place to start when a student has a real problem with an advisor. He or she will know the personalities of the people in the department and the standards and dynamics of the school, and may be helpful if he or she also has a reputation for keeping conversations in confidence.

Intervention

The best antidote to a negative or lukewarm evaluation is a positive one. Those who strongly support your candidacy can write particularly enthusiastic letters or make phone calls on your behalf. Conceivably they can, if willing, suggest to hiring institutions that one of your key recommenders is misjudging you. However, be extremely careful about an offer to do this on your behalf. Often any attempt to contradict criticism merely strengthens the hiring committee's impression that there must be something behind the controversy.

It is usually safer for your advocates merely to express enthusiasm for your candidacy, leaving employers free to form their own conclusions. Recommendations from those outside your department who know your work can be particularly helpful in this regard, as they obviously represent a different perspective.

Campus Credentials Services

Your career planning and placement office may offer you the valuable opportunity to keep a file of letters of recommendation which you can update easily and which are always immediately available. If it is the policy of your department to write new letters for each job a student applies for, you may want to have at least a backup file with the credentials service. Faculty go on sabbatical, get sick, or become extra busy and are not available to write customized letters for every job.

If you maintain a file of letters of recommendation, federal law gives you the option of maintaining nonconfidential letters to which you may have access. Generally these letters are not considered as credible as confidential ones.

Choosing the Materials to Send with an Application

Whatever you place on file, strengthen your presentation for a job by sending materials selectively. Even if your file contains many recommendations, don't send them all. Three or four strong letters are usually all you need. You may choose different subsets of recommendations depending upon the job's requirements.

Chapter 8
Learning About Openings

Once you have decided what kinds of jobs to pursue, there are several resources you can use to ensure that you learn about all the opportunities that might interest you.

Scholarly Associations

Every discipline has a scholarly association which serves its members in many ways. The association functions as the recorder and critic of scholarship in the discipline by producing one or more scholarly journals of refereed articles. Frequency of publication varies from journal to journal. These publications usually do not include job openings.

The association normally also holds a conference, usually on an annual basis, where the most recent research in the field is presented. There are many forms of conference presentation. Individual scholars, both Ph.D.'s and advanced graduate students, present papers they have prepared for the conference; groups of scholars participate in panel discussions; and individuals or research teams participate in poster sessions or other small group discussions of their work. Such conferences or conventions provide an opportunity for formal and informal communication on research and are crucial for keeping the discipline dynamic.

Scholarly associations also provide several job-related services. These range from listings posted on a bulletin board to very formal job markets where extensive interview schedules are the main means by which candidates obtain entry-level positions.

If you do not know which association is appropriate for your field ask your advisor, check the subject index of the latest edition of *National Trade and Professional Associations*, or check Appendix 2 of this book.

Job Listings

Most scholarly associations regularly publish a listing of postdoctoral and tenure-track academic job openings. When an academic department has an opening, it is customary to advertise the position in an association job newsletter. The institution pays the association a fee to place the advertisement.

In many cases, the job listings are available to members only. However, most associations offer membership to students at a reduced rate. Sometimes it is possible to subscribe to the job listings separately.

Your department probably receives the job listings from the corresponding association and possibly listings from related associations as well. Find out which job opening publications your department receives and where they are kept. Better still, get your own subscription. If it is not normally sent first class, find out whether it can be for an extra fee.

Job Placement

Most scholarly associations provide some kind of job placement program at their annual conventions. This can range from simply making interview rooms available, to maintaining notebooks or computer printouts of recent job openings, to running formalized placement operations with scheduled interviews for employers and candidates. Check with your association to see what kind of placement program it has. Of course, individual institutions also conduct interviews in their rooms or suites during conventions (see Conference and Convention Interviews).

Literature on Job Hunting

Some associations produce job hunting guides for their members. These can range from a single typed sheet of interviewing techniques to a published book covering all aspects of the job search in that field. Such guides often cover non-academic careers as well as academic employment. Appendix 2 lists association-produced guides.

Regional Associations

In addition to a regional chapter of your national association, you may find additional relevant local and regional associations. These usually have an annual meeting on a smaller scale and often offer some sort of job placement. Check with your advisor about these.

National and Local Publications

The Chronicle of Higher Education, the national newspaper of higher education, lists teaching positions across the United States as well as some international ones. Most college and university libraries and career planning offices receive it.

The opening and closing sections of the *Chronicle* contain reported articles on various aspects of higher education. Job openings are listed in "Bulletin Board," in the middle section of the *Chronicle*, in two ways: (1) an alphabetical listing by job title; and (2) display listings placed in no order, indexed by subject at the beginning of the section.

A fairly new publication is the bimonthly *Black Issues in Higher Education*, aimed at African-American and other minority academics. It has an extensive job listing section.

Never to be used as the sole source of job listings, but useful to those seeking part-time teaching jobs or positions in small two-year colleges, is the local newspaper employment section. Usually listed under "Education," and mixed in with educational administration and elementary and secondary teaching, are tenure-track teaching and adjunct faculty positions as well.

For non-tenure track jobs you should call departments that interest you. Such jobs are often not well publicized.

Your Network of People

Faculty in your department receive letters from colleagues at other schools where there are openings. Keep a high profile in your department so that they will think of you when they hear about jobs. Know where your department posts jobs and check there regularly.

Additionally, keep in touch with everyone you know who might hear about openings: for example, former graduate students who have already found jobs, former professors at other institutions, and people you have met at conferences. Let them know when you are beginning your job search and nearing the end of your dissertation. Be sure to thank anyone who notifies you of a job opening even if it doesn't work out or it is not a good fit for you.

Part III
Written Materials for the Search: Suggestions and Samples

Chapter 9
Responding to Position Announcements

When you apply for any college or university teaching position, you will be asked to submit a "curriculum vitae," a "vita," or a "c.v." All these terms apply to the same document, which is a summary of your education, experience, publications, and other relevant data. In addition you may be asked for a dissertation abstract, a summary of your future research plans, a chapter of your dissertation, or an entire research paper.

What is required varies from field to field. Check with your department to make sure that what you are sending is within the conventions. Sometimes you may find that job announcements ask that you "send credentials" or "send dossier." These terms do not have a standard meaning. You can usually assume that what is meant is a cover letter, a vita, and letters of recommendation. Sometimes a transcript is also required. Be guided by your department's advice about what is usual in your field. Probably the only way to be absolutely certain about what is desired by a given department that has used a vague phrase in its ad is to call and ask.

Sometimes application is a two-stage process, in which applicants initially send minimal information and some are further selected to send more detailed materials, such as a dissertation chapter. Use discretion in sending supporting materials that have not been requested.

Chapter 10
Vitas

Whether or not it is accompanied by letters of recommendation, your vita is always the first thing you will send to a hiring institution, whether it is called a "vita," a "c.v.," a "curriculum vitae," or, occasionally, a "résumé." In preparing it, your goal is to create enough interest in your candidacy that you are granted a personal interview. Design your vita so that your strongest qualifications stand out if an employer skims it for only a few seconds, and with enough supporting detail so that it will stand up to scrutiny during a thorough reading.

Getting Started

Before beginning to write your vita, review your educational and professional history. Using the categories suggested below, list everything which you can imagine could possibly be included. Eventually you will decide what to include or exclude, but begin by ensuring that you are not overlooking anything relevant. Write a draft, experiment with the format, eliminate irrelevant information, have the vita critiqued, and make at least one more draft before you produce the final version.

Organization and Content

A vita always includes your name; current address and telephone number; and information about your education, professional experience, publications, presentations, and honors. It may also include your permanent address and telephone number; professional, extracurricular, and community activities; professional memberships; foreign languages; and selected personal data. Your name, address, and telephone number(s) should appear at the top of the first page. After that, continue with "Education." Follow with categories in decreasing order of importance. One exception is publications; if you have a long list, convention usually places it at the end of your vita. Within each category, give information in reverse chronological order, from most recent backward. Be concise and use phrases, rather than complete sentences.

Name

Make sure that it appears on every page.

Address(es) and Phone Number(s)

Include both home and office numbers if available. Use only numbers at which you are sure that messages will be delivered reliably. An answering machine is a good investment. If you will be available at a number or address before or after a specific date, say so. Fax numbers and E-mail addresses, if you have them, are also useful inclusions.

Objective

A vita for a faculty or postdoctoral position, in contrast to a résumé for a non-academic position, typically does not include an "Objective," or statement of the type of position you want. A possible exception is the unusual situation in which your goals are very different from what most employers would imagine from your vita.

Education

Discuss your graduate and undergraduate work in detail. List each institution, degree, field of concentration, and date at which a degree was received. Search committees want to know when your dissertation will be finished, so indicate the anticipated date of completion. If you are just beginning your dissertation and preparing a vita for a fellowship or part-time position, you may want to include a date for the latest formal stage of graduate work you have completed ("Coursework completed, May 1991"; "Passed examinations with distinction, May 1991"; or whatever formal marker of progress your program may have).

Always include the title of your dissertation and the name of your advisor. You may include the names of committee members if you think their inclusion will be helpful to you. You may also list additional research projects or additional areas of concentration. You may include activities related to your graduate training; for example, "President, Graduate Chemistry Society." If you have been very active in graduate student government, you may wish to create a separate section entitled "Committees," or "University Service," which would appear after listings of more relevant academic detail. Do not include high school. If you want to include it in case alumni will recognize it, mention it briefly in a personal section at the end.

Honors

Whether you make this a separate section or a category under "Education" depends upon how important honors are in your qualifications. If you have received several prestigious and highly competitive awards, for example, you may highlight them in a separate section. On the other hand, if you have few honors, you probably do not want to call attention to that fact by creating a category with only one unimpressive entry.

Commonly known honors (Phi Beta Kappa) need no explanation, but other awards can be briefly explained. Foreign students, in particular, may want to stress the degree to which an unfamiliar award was competitive: for example, "One of three selected from among 2,000 graduating chemists nationally."

Experience

In this section, include all the experience that you now view as relevant to your professional objectives. For each position you have held, include the name of the institution with which you were associated, your responsibilities and accomplishments, dates, and, in most cases, your position title. Pick a format that you plan to use consistently. List positions or employers first in each entry depending on which format, on balance, shows you to best advantage. Sometimes a general heading of "Experience" will be appropriate, but frequently you will want to subdivide the section. A common division is "Teaching" and "Research."

Describe each item to give the reader an overview of what you did, together with details about the most interesting or impressive aspects of your position. Stress what you accomplished and uniquely contributed. Use verb phrases and make every word count. Thus, "Responsibilities included developing various new course materials and instructional aids," becomes "Developed syllabus and diagnostic exam later adopted by department."

If you are describing a research project, give a brief introductory statement indicating what you set out to accomplish and what results you obtained. This is not, however, the place for a complete dissertation abstract.

Professional Experience

If you are applying for a position in a professional school and have experience working in that profession, describe it.

Licensure/Registration/Certification

List these credentials for positions in professional schools in fields where they are required, for example: nursing, education, architecture.

Publications/Presentations

Although these are of extreme importance for an academic position, convention usually places them last once they have grown beyond a few entries. They are listed in standard bibliographic form for your field and may be subcategorized if you have a very long list. While it is acceptable to list articles as "submitted," or "in preparation," too many citations of this form not balanced by articles that are either published or in press can strike a pathetic note.

Be aware of prestige hierarchies, and don't dilute the credibility of presentations at established scholarly societies or articles in refereed journals by including term papers or publications in popular journals or newspapers. Separate refereed articles from anything else. Dissertations, even if microfilmed, are not usually considered publications unless they are subsequently published in a journal or as a book by a recognized publisher. Don't pad your publications list and don't include in it anything you would not want a hiring committee to read.

Grants

If you have received funding, list the funding agency, and the project(s) for which it was awarded. Candidates frequently list dollar amounts for major funded research projects. Usually you would list fellowship or dissertation support with "Honors." Occasionally a grant will appear in two sections of the vita. It may be listed briefly under "Honors," and the work it supported discussed in detail under "Experience."

Scholarly and Professional Memberships/Leadership

List memberships or committee work in scholarly or professional organizations. If you have been very active in university committee work, you might also include it here, or perhaps create a separate section to cover it. If you have organized or moderated conference sessions, this would be an appropriate place to say so.

Research Interests

This optional category is a list that gives a brief answer to the question: "What are your future research plans?" Interests listed here should be described at a level specific enough to be credible and general enough to indicate the direction your research might take over the next several years. You may also be asked to submit a brief (one or two page) discussion of your future research plans as a separate part of your application. Be prepared to discuss in detail anything that you put in this section.

Teaching Competencies

You may use this optional category if you feel that the areas you are qualified to teach are not entirely obvious from the rest of the entries in your vita. Its listings are more general than "Research Interests." Be careful not to list such a wide range of competencies that your list lacks credibility. If you list a subject as a teaching competency some other part of the vita should reinforce your qualifications to teach it. Be prepared to discuss your ideas about a syllabus/text for any course you list in this section.

Additional Information

Frequently called "Personal," this optional section may encompass miscellaneous information that does not fit elsewhere. You may include knowledge of foreign languages (if they are not very important to your research; if they are, you might give them their own section), extensive travel, and interests that you feel are important. If you worked prior to attending graduate school at jobs you now consider irrelevant, you may summarize them with a statement such as "Employment 1984–1987 included office and restaurant work." You need not include date of birth or a statement about your health. We recommend you do not include marital status unless you are sure it will work to your advantage to do so.

If anything in your vita may make an employer question whether you have United States work permission (for example, an undergraduate degree from another country), list United States citizenship or permanent residency if you have it. If you do not, either make the most positive statement you can about work eligibility, for example, "Visa status allows 18 months United States work permission," or omit any mention of citizenship.

References

List the people who write letters of recommendation for you and identify their institutions. Providing their telephone numbers is an added convenience to employers, if your recommenders are prepared for phone calls. Complete mailing addresses are not really necessary on the vita, because when written recommendations are required it is almost always your responsibility to see that they arrive. For this reason, the names of references are sometimes omitted on the vita.

Tailoring Your Vita to Its Audience

Your vita should always include basic information and the information you present should always be true. However, if you are applying for two distinct types of positions, or positions in different types of institutions and departments, you may wish to develop more than one version of your vita. Variations could include choosing headings to emphasize information of particular relevance to a situation (for example, including "Administrative Experience" for positions that involve both teaching and administrative components); giving details about additional areas of concentration more relevant to one field than another; and using different subsets of individuals to recommend you for different types of positions. Differences between versions of your vita are usually subtle, but can be effective nonetheless. Consider different versions if you are in an interdisciplinary field and will apply to more than one type of department.

Experienced Candidates

If you are several years past your first academic position, your vita will be longer than that of a new Ph.D. Its general appearance and construction, however, will be similar. Generally you will omit details about earlier experiences, while retaining mention of the experience itself. For example, your first vita may have given detail about what you did as a teaching assistant. Now you may merely list the position, without discussion of responsibilities. Your education will probably continue to remain at the top of the first page, although the amount of detail that you provide about it may diminish.

If entries in some of the categories in your vita are growing numerous, you may begin to introduce subdivisions. For example, publications may be divided among books, papers, and reviews. Your listings of professional associations may begin to include discussions of conference sessions that you moderated or organized.

Length

How long a vita may be varies from field to field. Check with your department. In any case, be as concise as possible. Many graduate students will be able to manage with not more than two pages, including publications. Naturally, the vitas of more experienced candidates will be longer.

Layout and Reproduction

Remember that you are designing your vita to capture your readers' attention at a first glance. Therefore pay attention to where you put information and how you format it. Try to organize the first page so that it contains the information about your greatest assets. That way the reader will be motivated to turn the page! In general, longer entries will call more attention to themselves than will shorter ones. Material near the top of the page will stand out more than that at the bottom. The left-hand column usually gets the greatest visual emphasis, so don't waste it with dates. Put dates on the right-hand margin, and use the left-hand margin for content items, such as names of institutions.

The advantages of using word processing to produce a vita are so great that you should plan to produce yours in this fashion even if you need to pay someone to do it for you. A word-processed, laser-printed document allows you to make slight changes or additions easily. It gives you the option of using fonts, which make the document look professional, and boldface, which is very helpful in highlighting information. Fonts smaller than 10 point are very difficult to read. Establish a consistent graphic hierarchy so that typeface for equivalent categories of information is the same. An example of one typical hierarchy appears below:

HEADING (for example, **EXPERIENCE**)
Important Item (for example, **University of Pennsylvania**)
Less Important Item (for example, *Teaching Assistant*)

Traditionally, typesetting of vitas has not been necessary, and some academic departments may have reacted negatively to it. On the other hand, the current availability of laser printers has given a more polished appearance to all materials used in the academic job search. Use conservative fonts and a laser printer.

Proofread your vita again and again. If it contains typographical or spelling errors, it can cause you to be dropped from consideration. To be doubly sure, ask a friend who is a good proofreader to read the draft also. Use a letter quality or laser printer for the original copy of your vita. Print it on good bond paper. Most photocopiers will not copy clearly onto bond, so have copies made by a printing service, or generate multiple copies on a laser printer. Paper may be white or cream. Do not staple pages together, but make sure your name and a page number appear on each page.

Help

Because a vita is often the first thing an employer sees of you, it is too important a document not to be thoroughly critiqued and revised. Show it to your advisor and others in your department. If your campus career planning and placement service has counselors who work with graduate students, they will also be glad to provide critiques and help you get your first draft together. To give your vita a good final test, show it briefly to someone who has not seen it and ask that person what he or she notices and remembers. If the most important items stand out, you're in good shape. Otherwise, more revision is in order.

A Note About the Sample Vitas Which Follow

The following examples, generously volunteered by real candidates, are provided to give you an idea of what such materials look like. Other than to omit the names of the authors, their advisors, committee members, and co-authors, we have tried to change them as little as possible. Occasionally some dates have been changed. The examples are arranged by field: humanities, social sciences, science/engineering, and professional disciplines, followed by the vita of a highly experienced candidate.

These examples should be regarded as excellent, but not necessarily perfect. They are not all in the same format, and they do not all subscribe to the same stylistic conventions, so that you can see there are many ways to construct a good vita. The custom in your own field, or an unusual combination of strengths in your background, might well dictate that your vita should be quite different in style, language, or appearance. Don't attempt to copy any single example. Rather, look at all of them to see which forms of presentation might suit your own taste or situation.

Sample Humanities Vita

ALYSSA CANDIDATE
Address
Phone Number

EDUCATION

University of X   Sept. 1985 - present
Philadelphia, PA
Ph.D. in Modern Hebrew and Arabic Literature, expected 1992
    Coursework in literary theory, evaluation, folklore
    Instituted a weekly lecture series through the Center for Middle East Studies
Dissertation: "Iraqi Israeli Writers: Exile from Exile"
    Committee: Advisor's Name, Committee Members' Names

Hebrew University   Sept. 1988 - July 1989
Jerusalem, Israel
    Visiting Graduate Student
    Graduate coursework in Hebrew literature, Arabic literature, and literary theory

American University in Cairo   June 1986 - June 1987
Cairo, Egypt
    Advanced study in Arabic language and literature
    Lecture course at the University of Cairo

University of Michigan   Sept. 1981 - May 1985
Ann Arbor, MI
    B.A. in Near East Studies: Hebrew with highest honors and highest distinction
    Hebrew University One Year Program

TEACHING EXPERIENCE

University of X
Modern Middle East Literature in Translation   1990
    Lecture and discussion with graded papers and essay exam
Modern Hebrew: first year   1989 - 1990
    Daily language class covering oral and written skills; emphasis on proficiency.
    Total responsibility for class, including curriculum and exam preparation.
Tutor, Arabic and Hebrew   1987 - 1988

Tahrir Home School, Cairo, Egypt   1986 - 1987
    Primary school English, mathematics and Arabic.

Alyssa Candidate - 2

AWARDS AND FELLOWSHIPS

Mellon Dissertation Fellowship (1991)
Annenberg Fellowship (1985-present)
Mellon Fellowship in the Humanities (1985-86; 1987-88)
Lady Davis Fellowship at Hebrew University (1988-89)
Rabbi Israel Goldstein Fellowship - honorary (1988-89)
Center for Arabic Study Abroad (CASA) Fellowship (1986-87)
Phi Beta Kappa (1985)
Metzger Award for Senior Honors Thesis (1985)
Underclass Honors Award (1983)
James B. Angell Scholar (1982)

PUBLICATIONS AND PRESENTATIONS

"Literature of the Ma'abarah," National Association of Professors of Hebrew, Yeshiva University, June 3-5, 1991.
"Samir Naqqash: Writer in Exile," American Comparative Literature Association, The Pennsylvania State University, March 29-31, 1991.
"Iraqi-Israeli Writers and the Choice of Language," Association for Jewish Studies, Boston, December 9, 1990.
Participating interviewer in literature, Project to Document the Heritage of Babylonian Jewry, Tel Aviv, Israel, May 14-17, 1990. Taped interviews stored in the archives at the Center for the Heritage of Babylonian Jewry, Or Yehuda.
"Language, Culture and Reality," *Alif: Journal of Comparative Poetics,* No.7, Spring 1988 [translation].
"The Folk Literature of Kurdistani Jews," *The Middle East and South Asia Folklore Newsletter*, Vol.3, No.2, Spring 1987 [book review].

PROFESSIONAL MEMBERSHIPS

National Association of Professors of Hebrew
Association for Jewish Studies
Middle East Studies Association
Modern Language Association
Association of American Teachers of Arabic
American Professors for Peace in the Middle East

Sample Humanities Vita

MICHELLE J. STUDENT
Address
Phone Number

EDUCATION

University of X, Philadelphia, Pennsylvania
Ph.D. Candidate, History (degree expected May 1990)
   Dissertation: "Popular Deities and Social Change during the Southern Song Period (1127-1270)"
   Dissertation Advisor: Advisor's Name
   Comprehensive exams passed with honors: Traditional and Modern Chinese History, South Asian History, Anthropology of Religion, May 1987.
M.A., History, 1986
   Coursework: Additional work in classical Chinese, Chinese popular religion, ethnohistory, historiography, Japanese (including two summers at Middlebury College, Vermont), Taoism, and social and cultural anthropology. Participated in the monthly ethnohistory colloquium sponsored by the History and Anthropology departments.

University of Kyoto, Kyoto, Japan, 1987-1989
   Fulbright-Hayes Fellow
   Affiliated with the East Asian History Department.
   Attended seminars run by Japanese scholars on Yuan history, epigraphic sources, and Chinese history.
   On two one-month trips to China, met with scholars and collected materials not available in Japan or the United States.

Inter-University Program for Chinese Language Study in Taiwan, 1982-1984
   (Stanford Center in Taipei).
   Devoted first year to intensive training in spoken Mandarin and classical Chinese. In second year, began Japanese while continuing Mandarin and classical Chinese.

Harvard University, Cambridge, Massachusetts
   B.A. magna cum laude, East Asian Studies, June 1982
   Senior thesis: "Mao and Gandhi and Their Relations with the Peasantry"
   Studied American, Chinese, Inner Asian, Japanese, and Latin American history as well as beginning Mandarin and classical Chinese.

HONORS AND FELLOWSHIPS

Mellon Dissertation Fellowship in the Humanities, 1989
Title VI Foreign Languages and Area Studies Fellowship, 1988
Fulbright-Hayes pre-doctoral fellowship for study in Japan and American Council of Learned Societies pre-doctoral grant, 1987
Dean's Fellowship, University of X, 1985
University Fellowship, University of X, 1984
Fulbright-ITT Fellowship for Chinese language study in Taiwan, 1982
Phi Beta Kappa, Radcliffe College, 1981

Michelle J. Student, 2

TEACHING EXPERIENCE

Teaching Fellow in Non-Western History, **University of X**, 1986-1987
o Conducted sections in African, Middle Eastern, Latin American, and South Asian history.
o Lectured on Chinese history.
o Writing-Across-the-University Fellow. Worked with students on an individual basis to improve their writing ability.

Private tutor in English as a Second Language in Boston's Chinatown, Taipei, and Kyoto, 1981-1989.

TEACHING COMPETENCIES

Survey courses in both world and non-Western history.
Advanced courses in Chinese, Japanese, and Indian history, covering both traditional and modern periods.

FOREIGN LANGUAGES

Strong reading knowledge of classical Chinese, modern Chinese, French, and Japanese. Fluent Japanese and Mandarin. Passed the State Department's interpreting exam in Mandarin.

RELATED WORK EXPERIENCE

Chinese-language visa interviewer at the U.S. Embassy, Taipei, 1983-1984
Tour guide in China, Summer 1987

PRESENTATIONS

"Popular Religion in the Southern Song: A look at Huzhou," April 1989
In Japanese at the Yuan History Seminar, Kyoto.

"Religious and Social Change in Hangzhou," May 1988
In Mandarin at the First International Conference on Song History, Hangzhou, China.

"Problems with the Song Sources about Popular Religion," December 1988
In Japanese at the graduate student colloquium, Kyoto University.

Sample Humanities Vita

MARGARET P. CANDIDATE

Home Address   Work Address
Telephone   Telephone

EDUCATION

UNIVERSITY OF X
Ph.D. in Romance Languages expected May 1986. Specialization in Medieval Religious Drama.
General emphasis on history and application of Rhetorical Theory. Experience with the University's
pilot pedagogical program in proficiency testing using FSI interview techniques.
Dissertation: "Rhetoric and the Origins of Medieval Drama in Arnoul Greban's *Mystère de la
Passion*." Director: Advisor's Name.

UNIVERSITY OF VIRGINIA
M.A. in French Literature, 1979
Master's Thesis: "La Logique des débats dans la Chanson de Roland." Director: Advisor's Name.
B.A. *summa cum laude* in French and Russian, 1977

UNIVERSITÉ DE PARIS III, 1975-76
Coursework toward the B.A. in French Literature.

INSTITUT DE LANGUES ET CIVILISATIONS ORIENTALES, 1975-76
D.E.U.G. curriculum in Russian Language and Linguistics.

PAPERS AND PUBLICATIONS

"Forensic Rhetoric and the Origins of Medieval Drama in Arnoul Greban's *Mystère de la Passion*."
International Congress on Medieval Studies, Kalamazoo. 10 May, 1986.

"Rhetoric and Dialect in Guido Cavalcanti's *Donna me Prega*." Accepted for publication in *Stanford
Italian Review*.

"The Rhetoric of Protestantism: Book I of Agrippa D'Aubigné's *Les Tragiques*," *Rhetorica* 3 (1985),
285-94. Earlier version presented at the MLA Convention, New York. 28 December 1981.

"The Logic of the Debates in the *Chanson de Roland*." MLA Convention, New York. 29 December
1981.

The Carvalho Collection: Documents and Manuscripts from the 11th to the 19th Centuries. In
collaboration with: Co-Authors' Names.

FELLOWSHIPS AND HONORS

Dean's Fellow in Medieval Studies. University of X, 1985-86
Dean's Scholar Award for Outstanding Scholarly Achievement. University of X, 1984. Awarded for
the first time to ten graduate students university-wide.
NEH Youth Grant. Romance Languages Editor for "The Carvalho Collection: A First Catalogue and
Exhibition." Principal duties included paleographical, philological, and historical analysis of French
and Belgian manuscripts and documents, medieval to modern. Philadelphia Free Library. Summer
1982.

M.P. Candidate - 2

Folger Shakespeare Library Fellowship to attend the seminar "The Origins of Medieval Drama" taught by Professor's Name and Professor's Name, Fall 1981.
University Fellow, University of X, 1980-81
Phi Beta Kappa, University of Virginia, 1977

TEACHING EXPERIENCE

UNIVERSITY OF X, 1984-85
Lecturer in French. Taught Advanced French Grammar to majors. Served as anchor person for the teaching of Elementary French with the Capretz method.

UNIVERSITÉ DE DIJON, 1982-84
Lecturer in English. Responsible for teaching courses in Conversation, Translation, Writing and Comprehension Skills, American Civilization, and Pronunciation. Experience in running Language Laboratory equipment. Assisted in the administration and operation of the Franco-American Club.

UNIVERSITÉ DE NANCY, 1984
Participated in the direction of the Télé-Enseignement Department's "American Civilization Day" held in Dijon. Joint follow-up included the creation of a series of language laboratory tapes on contemporary American civilization.

UNIVERSITÉ POUR TOUS DE BOURGOGNE, 1983-84
Designed and taught an Advanced English course for adults involving grammar review, conversation, and lab work.

LYCÉE SIMONE WEIL, Dijon, 1982-83
Taught Advanced English Conversation in a continuing education program.

UNIVERSITY OF X, 1981-82
Teaching Fellow in French. Taught at the Intermediate Level.

UNIVERSITY OF VIRGINIA, 1978-80
Teaching Assistant of Elementary and Intermediate French. Course co-coordinator for Intermediate Conversation, 1979-80.

RESEARCH IN PROGRESS

Ancient and modern rhetorical theory. The search for a common critical vocabulary to describe rhetoric's historical continuum in literature from *La Vie de St. Alexis* to Antonin Artaud.

The origins of medieval literary genres: anthropological and sociological approaches to language and literacy.

LANGUAGES

Command of Russian and Latin. Reading knowledge of German.

Sample Humanities Vita.
Candidate's work is creative, as well as scholarly.

ANN POET CANDIDATE
Address
Phone

EDUCATION

Ph.D., English, University of X, expected, 1991
M.A., Boston University, 1987
B.A., Yale University, 1984

DISSERTATION

Collage: An Approach to Reading African-American Literature
Director: Director's Name. [A short paragraph describing the dissertation follows.]

SCHOLARSHIPS, HONORS, AND FELLOWSHIPS

Scholar-in-Residence, Harverford College, 1990-91
Fellow, Corporation of Yaddo, August 1990
Fontaine Dissertation Fellowship, University of X, 1989-90
[Five additional honors follow.]

PUBLICATIONS

Books

The Venus Hottentot, Callaloo Poetry Series, University Press of Virginia, 1990.

Articles

Photo essay, co-authored with Name, in *Workings of the Spirit: A Poetics of Afro-American Women's Writing* by Houston A. Baker, Jr., University of Chicago Press (forthcoming Winter 1990).
[Two additional articles follow.]

Book Reviews

Collected Poems of Sterling Brown. Reviewed in *Village Voice Literary Supplement*, May 1990.
[Seven additional reviews follow.]

Poetry

"My Grandmother's Bathroom," "The Texas Prophet," and "Compass," in *Chelsea* (forthcoming, Winter 1990).
[Eleven additional poems follow.]

Fiction
"Pavo Real," *The American Voice* 12 (Fall 1988).
[Two additional citations follow.]

Ann Poet Candidate - 2

Additional

Articles in *The Washington Post* in OpEd, Editorial, Style, District Weekly, Religion, Outlook, and Book World sections.
[Additional citations appear.]

PAPERS READ

"Writing *The Venus Hottentot*," at American Literature Association Conference, San Diego, May 1990.
[Four additional papers follow.]

POETRY AND FICTION READINGS

Wesleyan University, as part of African-American Studies 1990-91 Lecture Series, November 1990.
[Many other readings follow.]

AWARDS

Nomination for 1990 Pushcart Prize for poetry
Nomination for two 1988 Pushcart Prizes for short fiction
1986 Larry Neal Writer's Award for Fiction, sponsored by the D.C. Commission on the Arts and Humanities
1984 James A. Veech Award for imaginative writing, Yale University

TEACHING EXPERIENCE

Haverford College, "Black Women's Literature: Images and College Self-Representation," (seminar), Fall 1990.
University of X, Freshman Composition: "Beyond the Blues: Reading Afro-American Poetry," Spring 1988; "Magical Realism in the U.S., Caribbean, and Latin America," Fall 1987
Germantown Friends School,"Beyond the Blues," Spring 1988 and 1989
Boston University, "Introduction to Creative Writing," Fall 1985

ACADEMIC ADMINISTRATION

Project Coordinator, Center for the Study of Black Literature and Culture, University of X, Summer 1988
Research Assistant in Afro-Hispanic Literature (Professor's Name), Yale University, 1983-84
Research Assistant, Black Periodical Fiction Project (Professor's Name), Yale University, 1982-84

TEACHING INTERESTS

Afro-American Poetry   Caribbean Literature
Afro-American Autobiography   Comparative Women's Narrative
Afro-American Culture Studies   19th and 20th century American poetry

REFERENCES. Please request dossier directly from me. I will have my university send it to you.

Sample Humanities Vita.
Candidate with administrative experience.

WALTER SCHOLAR

Work Address   Home Address
Telephone   Telephone

EDUCATION   Ph.D., History, University of Y, 1986
M.A., African History, University of Dar es Salaam, Tanzania, 1979
B.A., Black Studies and Political Science, Luther College, Decorah, IA, 1976

AWARDS AND HONORS

Fontaine Fellow, University of Pennsylvania, 1984, 1985
Fulbright Fellow, United Kingdom and Tanzania, 1983
University of Y Fellowship, 1979 - 1981
Fulbright Fellow, University of Dar es Salaam, 1977 - 1979
National Fellowship Fund Award (Ford), 1976 - 1977
Phi Beta Delta, Founder Member, 1990

EXPERIENCE

Teaching and Research

Lecturer, Department of History, University of Pennsylvania, Philadelphia, PA   1986 - Present

Guest Lecturer, Institute of African Studies, University of Ibadan, Nigeria, West Africa Summer 1988

Lecturer, Department of History, Rutgers University, Camden, NJ   Spring 1988

Researcher, Afro American Historical and Cultural Museum, Philadelphia, PA   Fall 1988

Fontaine Fellow, Visiting Pre-doctoral Fellow in History, University of Pennsylvania,
   Philadelphia, PA   1984 - 1986

Fulbright Fellow, United Kingdom and Tanzania, East Africa   1983

Fulbright Fellow, University of Dar es Salaam, Tanzania   1977 - 1979

Academic Administration

Director, African American Resource Center, University of Pennsylvania,   1989 - Present
   Philadelphia, PA

Walter Scholar, page 2

Faculty Master, DuBois College House, University of Pennsylvania, Philadelphia, PA	1986 - 1989
Faculty Director, Penn-in-Ibadan program, University of Pennsylvania, Philadelphia, PA	Summer 1988
Research Fellow, Afro-American Studies Program, University of Pennsylvania, Philadelphia, PA	1985 - 1989
Coordinator of African Resources and Curriculum, Department of History, University of Pennsylvania, Philadelphia, PA	1984 - 1985

PROFESSIONAL ACTIVITIES

Grant Reader, National Endowment for the Humanities, Washington, DC	June, 1990
Consultant, National Urban League of Philadelphia, Philadelphia, PA	May - June 1990
Panelist, National Association for Foreign Student Affairs, National Conference, Minneapolis, MN	June 1, 1989
Panelist, Inaugural Conference of Lincoln University's Center for Public Policy and Diplomacy, Lincoln University, Lincoln, PA	May 22 - 23, 1989
Keynote Speaker, AIM 21st Century Conference, SUNY-College at Old Westbury, Long Island, NY	May 1, 1989
Consultant/Instructor, Philadelphia Alliance for the Teaching of Humanities in the School, Philadelphia, PA	1986-present
Panelist, National Association for Foreign Student Affairs, Philadelphia, PA	November 1, 1988
Panelist, African Studies Association, Denver, CO	November, 1987
Panelist, African Studies Association, New Orleans, LA	November, 1985

COMMITTEE WORK

Affirmative Action Council
Provost Committee on Advising and Retention
Advisory Board, Office of International Programs
Ibadan Advisory Committee, Office of International Programs
African Studies Committee
Advisory Committee, James H. Robinson Internship in International Development, Operations Crossroads, Inc.

Sample Social Sciences Vita

HARI APPLICANT
Home Address
Home Telephone
Office Telephone

EDUCATION

University of X, Philadelphia, Pennsylvania
Candidate for Ph.D. in Economics

    Fellowships: Olin Fellowship (Law and Economics), 1988
                  Center for the Study of Organizational Innovation Research Fellow, 1986-87

    Fields of Concentration: Industrial Organization, Finance

Dissertation: "Three Essays on the Problems of Information in Financial Markets"
Supervisors: Name and Name
Expected Date of Completion: June 1989

University of Calcutta, India
    M.A., Economics, 1983

Presidency College, Calcutta, India
    B.A., Economics, Mathematics and English, 1980

EXPERIENCE

    Teaching Assistant, Law and Economics (undergraduate), Spring 1988
    Instructor, Introductory Microeconomics, University of X, Fall 1987, Summer 1988
    Teaching Assistant, Intermediate Macroeconomics, University of X, Spring 1987
    Instructor, Industrial Organization, University of X, Summer 1987
    Research Assistant to Name, University of X, Summer 1986
    Research Assistant to Name (currently at Rice University), 1984-1985

PUBLICATION

    "Testing for Aggregation Bias in Efficiency Measurement" (joint with Name and Name), in *Measurement in Economics*, edited by Name, Physica Verlag, Heidelberg, 1987

WORKING PAPER

    "Output Aggregation and the Measurement of Productive Efficiency" with Name and Name, Working Paper #87-6, Department of Economics, University of North Carolina, Chapel Hill, North Carolina, 1987

Hari Applicant - 2

UNPUBLISHED RESEARCH PAPERS

"Strategic Cost Over-Runs in a Bargaining Model with Uncertainty," mimeo, University of X, 1988
"Managerial Incentives, Disincentives and Takeovers," mimeo, University of X, 1988
"Piggybacking on Insider Trades," mimeo, University of X, 1988
"A Note on Second Mover Advantages Under Asymmetric Information," mimeo, University of X, 1988

RESEARCH INTERESTS

Industrial Organization: Bargaining, Research & Development, Product Differentiation
Finance: Asset Markets, Agency Problems, Empirical Research

TEACHING INTERESTS

Major: Industrial Organization   Minor: Game Theory
        Corporate Finance
        Microeconomics

PROFESSIONAL ACTIVITIES

Member, American Economic Association
Member, Econometric Society
Member, European Economic Association

REFERENCES

[Names, addresses, and phone numbers of six references follow.]

Sample Social Sciences Vita.
Candidate completed dissertation while working full-time.

ROGER RESEARCHER, Ph.D.

Office address and phone   Home address and phone

CURRENT POSITION

Research Sociologist and Director, Research Computer Services, Polisher Research Institute of the Philadelphia Geriatric Center, August 1986 to present. Member, Research Executive Committee.

EDUCATION

University of X, Ph.D., Sociology, August 1990.
Dissertation Title: The Psychological Well-Being of Elderly Jews: A Comparative Analysis. Committee: (Chair), (Members). **M.A., Sociology,** 1984. Teaching Fellowship 1981-1982.

Temple University, Urban Studies Program, 1976-1978. Graduate work in Sociology, Geography, Psychology and Urban Studies. **B.A. in American Studies,** *cum laude* with Honors, 1976.

TEACHING POSITIONS

Writing Fellow for "Writing Across The University" Program, University of X, Fall 1987.

Instructor in Sociology and **Social Psychology,** Gratz College, 1981 to 1987. Taught classes: "Anti-Semitism in America," "The Jewish Elderly."

Teaching Fellow, University of X, 1981-1982. Taught "Social Problems" in College of Arts and Sciences, and "American Society" in College of General Studies.

Teaching Assistant, University of X, 1979-1981. Assisted Name in "Social Stratification." Co-taught the class when the instructor became ill in 1979. Graded exams through Spring 1990. [Two additional positions are listed.]

RESEARCH/ADMINISTRATIVE POSITIONS

Research Sociologist and Director, Research Computer Services, Polisher Research Institute, Philadelphia Geriatric Center, August 1986 to Present. **Research Associate for Computers and Statistics,** April 1985 to August 1986. **Research Assistant,** June 1984 to April 1985.

Guest Archivist, Germantown Historical Society, January to June 1984. Organized collection of deeds and manuscripts related to purchases of land in Germantown area over a period of 300 years.

Research Analyst, Center for Research on the Acts of Man: 1979, 1981. Data analysis for studies of energy use by individuals of differing economic status and of the impact of industrialization on Inuit Eskimos.

Principal, M. E. Kalish School, 1977-1982. Established curriculum and hired and trained teachers.

PUBLICATIONS: JOURNAL ARTICLES

Name; Name; Name; Roger Researcher and Name. "A Two-Factor Model of Caregiving Appraisal and Psychological Well-Being." Journal of Gerontology: Psychological Sciences. In press. [Many other publications follow.]

Roger Researcher, Ph.D., 2

PUBLICATIONS: OTHER

Researcher, Roger. "The Elderly" in Encyclopedia of Jewish American History and Culture.   In press.
[Many additional publications follow.]

ACADEMIC PRESENTATIONS

Researcher, Roger. "American Jews and Caregiving for the Aged." 21st Annual Meeting of the Association for Jewish Studies, Boston: December 1989.
[Many other presentations follow.]

SELECTED OTHER PRESENTATIONS

"Considerations in Selecting Computer Systems in Long-Term Care Facilities." Pre-Conference Workshop on Computers and Long-Term Care at the 42nd Annual Scientific Meeting of the Gerontological Society of America, November 1989.
[Many other presentations follow.]

INTERNATIONAL ACTIVITIES

Scholar-in-Residence, Brookdale Center on Aging and Human Development, Jerusalem, July 1989.
[A presentation at an international convention is also listed.]

GRANTS AWARDED

Co-Investigator, Designing a Clinical Psychology Database Structure. November 1987 to July 1988. Principal Investigator: Name. Other co-investigators: Names. NIH Biomedical Small Grant Award.

WORK IN PROGRESS

Selected to complete a monograph on the Jewish elderly based on data collected in the 1990 National Jewish Population Survey. Completing work on a grant proposal concerning the impact of cultural background on aging for the National Institute on Aging.

MEMBERSHIPS

[Several memberships are listed].

PROFESSIONAL ACTIVITIES

Member, Executive Board of the Association for the Social Scientific Study of Jewry, 1990-1992. Co-Editor (with Name) Newsletter of the Association for the Social Scientific Study of Jewry, 1987 to present.
Chair, Session on Sociological Studies of the American Rabbinate, co-sponsored by the Association for the Social Scientific Study of Jewry, 22nd Annual Meeting of the Association for Jewish Studies Boston: 1990.
[Many other activities follow.]

COMMUNITY ACTIVITIES

Participate in a variety of community sponsored activities including serving on boards and public speaking, as well as taking a leading role in charitable activities. Received awards for community service.

Sample Social Sciences Vita

SHASTRI PROFESSIONAL

Address   Telephone (H)

EDUCATION

University of X, Philadelphia, PA
Ph.D, Social Psychology, December, 1989
  Dissertation: A Study of the Interrelationships among Belief Systems: Religious,
                  Control, and Justice
  Advisor: Dr. Name

Drexel University, Philadelphia, PA
M.S., Organizational Behavior, 1978

Tata Institute of Social Sciences, Bombay, India
M.A., Family and Child Study, 1974
  Thesis: Title

Maharaja Sayajirao University, Baroda, India
B.Sc., Major: Child Development, 1972

TEACHING EXPERIENCE

Teaching Assistant, University of X, Philadelphia, PA, 1983-1987
Undergraduate course on Life Span Human Development.

Visiting Lecturer, Cumberland County College, Millville, NJ, 1985
Taught freshman level courses in General Psychology and Life Span Human Development.

Guest Instructor, Maharaja Sayajirao University, Baroda, India, March 1985
For Faculty of Management, conducted workshops in group dynamics focusing on
interpersonal awareness, power, authority, and conflict and competition.

Visiting Lecturer, County Vocational Technical Institute, Bridgeton, NJ, 1980-1983
Taught psychology of aging and issues of mental health in the aged.

TEACHING INTERESTS

General Psychology
Life Span Human Development
Cross-Cultural Social Psychology
Graduate seminar in Cultural Social Psychology
Interested in teaching Group Dynamics and Organizational Behavior.

Shastri Professional - 2

RESEARCH EXPERIENCE

Graduate Research with Dr. Name, 1983-present
Studied the interaction and effect of ethno-religious groups on religious and secular beliefs of Hindus, Muslims, and Christians in India (1985). Studied the effect of socio-economic class on religious beliefs about God, soul, and evil, and secular beliefs such as ESP (1984).

Graduate Research with Dr. Other Name, 1989
Statistical analysis of data on mentor relationship and professional advancement of female employees in a corporation.

[Three additional positions are listed.]

RESEARCH INTERESTS

Influence of life events on three belief systems: religious, control, and justice.
Cultural determinants of attribution of responsibility for various fortunate and unfortunate events, and also injustices.
Concept of evil and various cultural defenses about the belief.

OTHER PROFESSIONAL EXPERIENCE

Clinical, Center for Human Development, Millville, NJ, 1978-1983
Outpatient, individual, and group therapy; supervised counselors and managed a clinical residence program. Provided emergency psychiatric consultation. (part-time 1983-1985)

PAPERS

[Several are listed.]

PRESENTATIONS

Professional, Shastri, and Name. "Religious and Secular Beliefs of Hindus, Muslims, and Christians of Different Economic Status," Conference of Society of Cross-Cultural Research, in Miami, FL (February 13, 1987).

PROFESSIONAL MEMBERSHIPS

[Several are listed.]

Permanent U.S. resident.

Sample Science/Engineering Vita

SARA SMITH-RESEARCHER

Work Address
Work Phone
E-Mail Address

EDUCATION

Harvard Medical School
Boston, Massachusetts
NIH Post-doctoral Research Fellow (1990-1992)
Advisor: Advisor's Name
Project: Investigation of the Biosynthesis of Enterobactin

University of X
Philadelphia, Pennsylvania
Ph.D. in Organic Chemistry (Spring 1990)
Advisor: Professor Name
Thesis: "Progress Toward the Total Synthesis of Acutiphycin."
GPA: 3.9/4.0

State University of New York at Buffalo
Buffalo, New York
B.S. in Chemistry (1984)
Undergraduate Research Advisor: Professor Person
Assisted with work leading to the total synthesis of arteannuin B.
GPA: 3.6/4.0

Erie Community College
Williamsville, New York
A.A.S. in Chemical Technology (1980)
GPA: 3.9/4.0

EXPERIENCE

FMC Corporation
Agricultural Chemical Division
Princeton, New Jersey
Summer 1983 and 1984
Responsible for the synthesis, isolation purification, and characterization of compounds with potential biological activity as pesticides.
Supervisors: Dr. Science (Summer 1984)
Dr. Investigator (Summer 1983)

Sara Smith-Researcher, 2

FMC Corporation
Agricultural Chemical Division
Middleport, New York
1980-1982
> Responsible for the synthesis, isolation purification, and characterization of compounds with potential biological activity as herbicides.
> Supervisor: Dr. Name

OFFICES AND AWARDS

Eli Lilly Travel Award (1989)
Association for Women in Science Pre-doctoral Award (1989)
Workshop Leader: Training Program for Teaching Assistants (Fall 1988 and 1989)
President, Chemistry Department Graduate Student Activities Council (1986-1987)
Distinguished Organic Chemistry Teaching Award (1985)
Chemical Association of Western New York Award (1982)

SOCIETIES

Phi Beta Kappa
Phi Lambda Upsilon
American Chemical Society

PUBLICATIONS

Name, Name, Name, Smith-Researcher, S., Name (1991). "Biosynthesis of the E.coli Siderophore Enterobactin: Sequence of the entF gene, Expression and Purification of EntF, and Analysis of Covalent Phosphopantetheine," *Biochemistry* (in press).

Smith-Researcher, S., Name, Name, Name (1991). "Synthesis of the C(3)-C(11) Fragment of the Cytotoxic Macrolide Acutiphycin: Stereocontrolled [2,3]-Sigmatropic Rearrangement of a Tertiary Allylic Ether," *Tetrahedron Letters* (manuscript in preparation).

REFERENCES

[Names, addresses, and phone numbers of three references are listed.]

Sample Science/Engineering Vita

MARIA L. CANDIDATE
Address   Home Phone Number   Laboratory Phone Number

EDUCATION

University of X, Department of Biology, Philadelphia, PA
Ph.D. in Cell and Developmental Biology, May 1990
Honors: NIH Training Grants in Cardiovascular Research (1985 - 1988) and Analysis
Development (1987 - present), Head Teaching Fellow (1985)

University of California at Los Angeles (UCLA), Zoology Department
M.A. in Developmental Biology, December 1982
Honors: Teaching Fellowship, NSF Fellowship (1981, declined)

Russell Sage College, Troy, NY
B.A. in Biology, May 1981
Honors: Kellas Scholar, Class of 1975 Chemistry Award, Wilson Award in Biology (1977), NY
State Regents Scholarship, Panhellenic Scholarship

EXPERIENCE

Research

Postdoctoral Fellow, **Thomas Jefferson Medical College**, Daniel Baugh Institute, Department of
Anatomy, Philadelphia, PA
Biochemical studies on hormonally induced cAMP mediated intracellular transduction mechanisms
involved in murine palate development: kinetic analysis of ligand-receptor binding of
cAMP-dependent protein kinase; intracellular localization and translocation of the enzyme regulatory
subunits upon hormonal stimulation; and cAMP-dependent protein kinase regulation of ornithine
decarboxylase induction.
Skills and Methodology: Radioligand-receptor binding studies; subcellular fractionation;
DEAE-column chromotography; fluorometric analysis; tissue culture and cell fusion. Laboratory of
Name (1990 - present).

Doctoral Dissertation, **University of X**, Departments of Biology and Anatomy
Research on the regulatory role of extracellular matrix molecules in directional migration of
precardiac cells during early heart organogenesis. Advisor's Name (1984 - 1990)
Skills and Methodology: Tissue culture; microsurgery; monoclonal antibody technology;
immunohistochemistry; scanning and transmission electronmicroscopy; phase and fluorescence
microscopy; protein purification techniques, including polyacrylamide gel electrophoresis, affinity
chromotography, and Western blots; computer-assisted image analysis and data processing.
Studies on microtubule organizing centers utilizing cell fractionation techniques.

Research Assistant, **University of Southern California Medical School**, Department of Pathology,
Los Angeles, CA
Research on immunologic mechanisms in oncology including induction and transfer of
immunological factors between sensitive and insensitive murine strains (1983).
Methodology: DNA purification; tissue culture techniques, including Rose Chambers Leighton tubes.

Master's Research, **University of California at Los Angeles**, Zoology Department
Studies on changes in protein synthesis during development, using polyacrylamide gel
electrophoresis and biochemical analyses (1981 - 1982).

Maria Candidate - 2

Senior Honors Research, **Russell Sage College**, Biology Department, Troy, NY
Analyzed the genetic expression of eye pigments in various mutants of the miniature wasp, **Habrobracon**, using chromatographic and spectrophotometric techniques (1980 - 1981).

Teaching

Lecturer, **University of X**, College of General Studies
Organized and taught: Cell and Molecular Biology. Supervised and coordinated two graduate teaching assistants' activities in laboratory (Summer 1987).
Advanced Developmental Biology (Fall 1989 - present).

Teaching Fellow, **University of X**, Department of Biology, Laboratory of Cell and Molecular Biology course (1984 - 1985); **University of X**, School of Veterinary Medicine, Laboratory in Embryology (Fall 1987, 1988, 1989), Lectured section on early heart development and assisted students in studies of serial sections of mammalian embryology; **University of California at Los Angeles**, General Biology and Developmental Biology (1981 - 1983).

Instructor, **Holy Family College**, Biology Department, Philadelphia, PA
Organized and taught courses and laboratories in various disciplines: Developmental Biology, Genetics, Microbiology, Histology.
General Biology taught at several levels: for majors, for nursing and medical technology majors, and for elementary education majors (1979 - 1983).

Administrative

Coordinator, Analysis of Development Seminar Series, **University of X**, Philadelphia, PA
Selected speakers, arranged for seminar presentations by internationally known scientists, and organized speakers' activities while on campus (1987 - 1989).

Head Teaching Fellow, **University of X**, Department of Biology
Supervised and coordinated activities of eight teaching assistants in Cell and Molecular Biology course (Fall 1985).

Evaluation Committee Member, **Holy Family College**, Biology Department, Philadelphia, PA
Aided in evaluation of department's present curriculum and projections of future needs for Middle Atlantic States accreditation. Committee's projections led to development of successful Nursing Department at the College (1974).

[A page of **PUBLICATIONS**, divided by **Papers** and **Abstracts**, follows.]

Sample Science/Engineering Vita

SANJAY APPLICANT
Work Address
Work Phone

EDUCATION

Ph.D., University of X, Department of Systems, Philadelphia, Pennsylvania, May 1990
Major Fields: Operations Research and Network Analysis
Thesis: "A Dynamical Systems Perspective for Mathematical Programming"
Supervisor: Name
Co-Supervisor: Name

B.E., University of Bombay, Electrical Engineering, 1986

PROFESSIONAL EXPERIENCE

Research Fellow, Network Analysis Laboratory, University of X   1988-present
Developed theory and computational methods for modeling very large scale networks with applications
to transportation, logistics and telecommunications. Developed AI techniques for solving Stackelberg
games on networks. Applied these models to the study of transportation infrastructure investment
policies in Africa and the Middle East.

Teaching Assistant, Department of Electrical Engineering, University of X   1987
Taught a recitation section for an undergraduate course in electrical circuits. Also assisted in the
preparation and grading of exams.

Product Development Assistant, Bombay Electronics   Summer, 1985
Received training in digital systems and microprocessors. Developed several measurement instruments
and designed a technical training system.

PRIZES AND AWARDS

Nominated for Sigma Xi membership, 1990
UPS Foundation Doctoral Fellowship, 1989-1990
[Several additional prizes are listed.]

RESEARCH INTERESTS

Transportation network design
Dynamic equilibrium of transportation networks
Very large scale freight/logistics network models
Network models
Combinatorial optimization
Game theory
Dynamical systems
Interior point methods (including Karmarkar's algorithm)
Sensitivity analysis of linear and nonlinear programs

SELECTED COURSEWORK

Advanced Transportation Network Analysis
Network Analysis
Facility Location on Networks
Optimization Theory
Game Theory and Mathematical Economics
Graph Theory and Integer Programming
Combinatorics and Graphs
Linear Systems

PUBLICATIONS

"Sensitivity Analysis Based Heuristics for Mathematical Programs with Variational Inequality Constraints," with Name, Name, and Name. *Mathematical Programming*, Series B (To appear, 1990).

"A Simulated Annealing Approach to the Network Design Problem with Variational Inequality Constraints," with Name, Name, Name, and Name. *Transportation Science* (Being revised after favorable review)
[Three additional publications are listed.]

CONFERENCE PRESENTATIONS

"The Generalized Metropolis Algorithm and its Applications to Simulated Annealing," with Name and Name. ORSA/TIMS, New York, 1989

"A Dynamical Systems Perspective for Mathematical Programming," with Name, Name, and Name. SIAM Conference on Dynamical Systems, Orlando, 1990

Invited to co-chair a session on Multicriteria Decision Making Applications in Natural Resources at the Ninth International Multicriteria Decision Making Conference, Fairfax, Virginia, August 1990

[Two additional presentations are listed.]

PROFESSIONAL SOCIETIES

Operations Research Society of America
Mathematical Programming Society
The Institute of Management Science
Society for Industrial and Applied Mathematics
American Mathematical Society
Institute of Electrical and Electronics Engineers

Sample Science/Engineering Vita

T.R. RESEARCHER

Address
Phone

EDUCATION

UNIVERSITY OF X, Philadelphia, PA
School of Engineering and Applied Science
Candidate for Doctor of Philosphy in Bioengineering, December 1989
 Dissertation: "The Genesis of the Intramyocardial Pressure and Ventricular Transmural
 Dynamics"
 Developed various mathematical models, including a model of the contracting myocyte to be
 used as the building block of a global model of the left ventricle.
 Advisor: Professor Name
Master of Science in Bioengineering, May 1986.
 Examined the effect of vascular peripheral resistance on the Kofotkoff Sound.
Bachelor of Science in Engineering, cum laude, May 1985.
 Chosen for early matriculation into master's program.

RESEARCH EXPERIENCE

CARDIOVASCULAR STUDIES UNIT, UNIVERSITY OF X
Research Associate. Developed computer models to explore the role of intramyocardial pressure as
a determinant of extravascular resistance (1984-present).
Research Assistant. Investigated the effect of arterial visco-elasticity and the sphygmomanometer
design on blood pressure measurement (1982-1984).

LIKOFF CARDIOVASCULAR INSTITUTE, HAHNEMANN UNIVERSITY
Research Associate. Conducted open chest experiments on canines to examine transmural
intramyocardial dynamics. Assisted in procedures involving left ventricle assist devices (1987-present).

ULTRASOUND SUITE, BROOKDALE HOSPTIAL
Laboratory Assistant. (Summer 1982).

TEACHING EXPERIENCE

DEPARTMENT OF BIOENGINEERING, UNIVERSITY OF X
Teaching Assistant. Assisted in development and taught a junior level biomedical instrumentation
laboratory course. Responsible for design of experiments and grading of lab reports (1988-1989).
Organized a computer laboratory for bioengineering department (Fall 1987).
Senior Design Supervisor. Developed and advised on undergraduate student's engineering design
thesis project (1986-1987).
Freshman Project Advisor. Designed and supervised innovative clinically oriented projects for
bioengineering students (1983-1987).
Private Tutor. Tutored college students in calculus courses (1983-1987).

T.R. Researcher - 2

ADMINISTRATIVE EXPERIENCE

DEPARTMENT OF RESIDENTIAL LIVING, UNIVERSITY OF PENNSYLVANIA
Head Resident. Advanced from position of Resident Advisor to Head Resident. Designed and developed a new freshmen housing project. Interviewed, selected, trained, and supervised a staff of four resident advisors. Implemented cultural, educational, and social programs for a Graduate Student Complex. Enforced disciplinary procedures and balanced fiscal budget (1984-1989).

ACADEMIC/PROFESSIONAL HONORS

Training Grant, University of X
National Institute of Health Research Fellowship
Louisiana Technical University Founder Scholarship for Outstanding Achievement in Biomedical Engineering Studies
Mortar Board Senior Honor Society
Atlantic Regional Inter-League Mathematics Competition
Gold Medal in the Nassau County Interscholastic Mathematics League

SCIENTIFIC/PROFESSIONAL AFFILIATIONS

Biomedical Engineering Society (BMES)
Cardiovascular System Dynamic Society (CSDS)
The Graduate Association in Bioengineering (GABE)
The Institute of Electrical and Electronics Engineers (IEEE)

CONFERENCE PRESENTATIONS

Association for Advancement of Medical Instrumentations, Washington, DC (April 1984)
CSDS VIth International Conference, Philadelphia, PA (October 1984)
CSDS VIIth International Conference, Zuoz, Switzerland (August 1986)
Academy of Surgical Research, Clemson, SC (October 1986)
Northeast Bioengineering 13th Annual Conference, Philadelphia, PA (March 1987)
FASEB 72nd Annual Meeting, Las Vegas, NV (May 1988)
CSDS IXth International Conference, Halifax, Nova Scotia, Canada (November 1988)

PUBLICATIONS

Researcher, T., Name, Name, and Name. (1984) The Effect of Peripheral Resistance on the Korotkoff Sound: Experiments. Proceedings of 19th Annual Meeting, Association for Advancement of Medical Instrumentation, Washington, DC, 68.

Researcher, T., Name, Name, and Name. (1984) Transmural Pressure-Flow Relations. Proceedings of VIth International Conference, Cardiovascular System Dynamics Society, Philadelphia, PA, 193-196.

[Many additional publications are listed.]

Sample Professional School Vita

MARK BRECKENRIDGE APPLICANT

Current Position
Current Employer
Current Employer's Address
Work Phone

EDUCATION

University of X, The Business School, 1989
Doctor of Philosophy in Risk and Insurance. Secondary Emphasis in Finance.
Dissertation: *Interest Rates and the Value of Capital: Duration Mismatch in the Property Liability Insurance Industry*

University of California at Berkeley, 1980
Master of Business Administration, Finance and International Business
Thesis: *The Impact of Inflation on the Value of Ordinary Whole Life Insurance*

Brigham Young University, 1978
Bachelor of Arts in Economics. High Honors Designation.

ACADEMIC POSITIONS

Institut Européen d'Administration des Affaires (INSEAD), Fontainebleau, France
Assistant Professor of Finance, September 1989-present.

The Business School, University of X, Philadelphia, Pennsylvania
Lecturer, Insurance Department, September 1988-June 1989.

California State University, Hayward, California
Lecturer, Finance Department (evening M.B.A. Programme), 1979-1980.

Institute for Business and Economic Research, University of California, Berkeley, California
Research Associate, 1979-1980.

PUBLICATIONS AND CURRENT RESEARCH

"A Capital Budgeting Analysis of Life Insurance Costs in the United States, 1950-1979," Journal of Finance, March 1983. (Co-author with Name).

"Engel Curve Analysis of Gambling and Insurance in Brazil," Journal of Risk and Insurance, September 1983. (Co-author with Name).

"The Market Reward for Insurers that Practice Asset/Liability Management," Financial Institutions Research, Goldman Sachs. November 1989. (Co-Author with Name).

M.B. Applicant - 2

"Interest Rates and Value of Capital: Duration Mismatch in the Property Liability Insurance Industry."
Unpublished Working Paper, 1990. (Co-Author with Name).
[Five additional publications follow.]

PROFESSIONAL EXPERIENCE

Continental Asset Management (Continental Insurance Corp.), New York
Consultant. Analyzed the impact of interest rates changes on the duration mismatch of asset and liability
portfolios (and resultant impact on the market value) of property liability insurers. 1988-Present.

United States General Accounting Office, Washington, DC
Financial Economist. General Government Division, Insurance Group. Principal projects included a
comprehensive study of the role of the U.S. government as lender of last resort and an analysis of the
expanding use of financial guarantees in the insurance industry. 1985-1986.

Crocker National Bank, San Francisco, California
Deputy Representative. Santiago, Chile Representative Office.
Responsible for the financial analysis of the bank's portfolio in the public, financial, and corporate
sectors; marketed operational and trade related services to correspondent banks; negotiations with Chilean
government officials regarding debt restructure; profitability planning and expense control. Laid
groundwork for opening Santiago Representative Office. During 1984 served as acting representative
with full responsibility for the country management of Chile and with additional responsibilities for Peru
and Bolivia. 1982-1985.

Planning and Control Unit. International Division.
Responsible for Latin American and European area. Initiated and coordinated computerization of
profitability tracking systems. 1980-1981.

PROFESSIONAL AFFILIATIONS

American Economics Association
American Finance Association
American Risk and Insurance Association
European Network in Financial Markets (European Science Foundation)
European Group of Risk and Insurance Economists (Geneva Association)
Financial Management Association

PERSONAL DATA

Citizenship: U.S.A.
Languages: English, Spanish (fluent), French (fair), Danish (some)
Interests: History, art, travel, camping, and backpacking
Status: Married, two children. [Note: Including family status is appropriate here, as candidate now
works in Europe, where it is more frequently listed.]

Sample Professional School Vita

MEHRI ASPIRANT
Address
Home Telephone/Work Telephone

EDUCATION
> **University of X**, Graduate School of Fine Arts, Philadelphia, PA
> **Ph.D. in Architecture**, 1990
> Major: Architectural Technology
> Dissertation: "Buildings as Cyborgs: Expressions of Hand and Machine Craftsmanship in Architecture"
> Committee Members: Supervisor's Name, Other Name, Other Name
> **M.S. in Architecture**, 1986
> Major: Theories of Architecture and Technology (GPA = 3.6/4.0)

> **Massachusetts Institute of Technology**, School of Architecture and Planning, Cambridge, MA
> **S.M. ARCH.S.**, 1984
> Major: Building Systems (GPA = 4.8/5.0)
> Thesis: "A Normative Approach to the Evaluation of Industrialized Building Systems"
> Committee Members: Advisor's Name, Other Names

> **Harvard University**, Graduate School of Design, Cambridge, MA, 1983-1984

> **University of Baghdad**, College of Engineering, Department of Architecture, Baghdad, Iraq
> **B.Sc. in Architecture**, magna cum laude, 1980

ACADEMIC/PROFESSIONAL HONORS
> The Willard A. Oberdick Fellowship in the Building Sciences, University of Michigan, Ann Arbor (1990-1991)
> ACSA Construction Materials and Technology Institute Fellowship, University of New Mexico, Albuquerque (August 1990)
> [Four additional honors follow.]

TEACHING EXPERIENCE
> Visiting Assistant Professor: College of Architecture and Urban Planning, University of Michigan (Fall 1990-present)
> Teaching Assistant: Graduate School of Fine Arts, University of X (1985-1989)
> Lecturer: University of X (1985-1989), New Jersey Institute of Technology (Spring 1988)
> Instructor: Elective Week (Case Studies in the Evolution of Building Types), Graduate School of Fine Arts, University of X (Fall 1986)
> Guest Critic: Master of Architecture Design Studios, Department of Architecture, University of X (Fall 1984, 1988)
> Guest Lecturer: Master of Architecture Program, MIT (Spring 1984), Graduate School of Design, Harvard University (Fall 1982)

TEACHING INTERESTS
> Building Materials: Properties and Applications
> History and Theories of Technology
> Processes of Building Production and Construction
> Technology Transfer: Past and Present
> Evolution of Building Types
> Architecture and Planning of the Non-Western World

RESEARCH EXPERIENCE
Post-Doctoral Fellow: College of Architecture and Urban Planning, University of Michigan (1990-present)
Researcher/Archivist: G. Robert Le Ricolais Collection at the Architectural Archives at the University of X (1988-1990)
Research Assistant: Doctoral Program in Architecture, University of X (1985-1989)
Assistant Coordinator/Researcher: Aga Khan Program for Islamic Art and Architecture, Harvard University and MIT (1982-1984)
Assistant Researcher: Scientific Research Council, Baghdad (1980-1982)

RESEARCH INTERESTS
Theories of Technology: Appropriate Technology and Its Applications, Architectural Technology, Building and Construction, Building Systems, Building Materials, Hand and Machine Production, Industrialization, and High-Tech
Houses and Housing: Theory, Design, and Building
Theories of Architecture: 19th and 20th Century
Architectural Education: Theory and Practice
Cross-Cultural Issues: History, Science, and Technology

PROFESSIONAL PRACTICE
Architect: Central Consultant, Baghdad (1977-1982)
Project Manager and Architect: Building Unit, Building Research Center, Baghdad (1980-1982)
Assistant Architect: University of Baghdad Engineering Consulting Firm, Baghdad (1981-1982)
Draftsperson: Ministry of Housing and Public Works, Baghdad (Summer 1978)

PROFESSIONAL AFFILIATIONS
Building Arts Forum/New York, Member (1989)
Architectural Union/Baghdad, Registered Architect (1980)
Engineering Society/Baghdad, Member (1980)

PUBLICATIONS/RESEARCH PAPERS
"Interpreting Architecture Through Technology: A Tale of Two Buildings," Proceedings of the ACSA West Regional Meeting, Denver, Colorado (October 1990)
[Twelve additional publications are listed.]

PUBLIC SERVICE
Orientation Coordinator: Graduate School of Fine Arts, University of X (1988, 1989)
Lecturer: World Affairs Council of Philadelphia (1988-1989)
Facilitator/Coordinator: Partnership for Professional Development, Philadelphia (1987-1989)
Chairperson: Ph.D. Architecture Students Committee, University of X (1984-1987)
Representative: Architectural Technology Group, MIT (1982-1984)

PERSONAL
Head Resident: On-Campus Graduate Students Housing, University of X (1986-1989)
Part-time Assistant: Ph.D. Program in Architecture Office, University of X (Fall 1984-Fall 1987)
Participated in the Paris Program, University of X (Summer 1985)
Verbal and written fluency in Arabic, working knowledge of French and Italian.

Sample Professional School Vita

TAMARA APPLICANT
Address
Home Phone Number

EDUCATION

Ph.D., University of X, Reading, Writing, Literacy, 1990
M.S. Ed., University of X, Secondary English Education, 1974
B.A., University of X, General Literature, 1973

Dissertation: "Talk About Writing and The Revision of Rough Drafts"
Committee Chair's and Committee Members' Names

HONORS AND AWARDS

Ph.D. conferred with distinction, University of X, 1990
Advisor to Literary Magazine: Columbia Scholastic Press Association, first place winner, 1987; NCTE, Superior Rating, 1987
Phi Beta Kappa
[Two additional honors follow.]

TEACHING EXPERIENCE

Assistant Professor, University of X
Freshman Composition, 1990-present and 1982-83.
Reading, Writing, and Critical Thinking, for degree-granting program for corporate employees, 1991.

Instructor, Beaver College
Taught Developmental Reading to Graduate Students, 1990-present.

Teacher, Akiba Academy
Designed and taught 8th grade ethnic studies curriculum; 11th grade American Literature, 12th grade electives: 1920's American Literature, Southern Writers, and Writers' Workshop, 1974-89.

Tutor of adolescents and adults in reading, writing, study and test-taking skills. Conferred with individuals on writing (college application essays, dissertations, professional presentations). Developed private tutoring/editing business; developmental issues, learning styles and disabilities, 1984-present.

Lecturer, Harcum Junior College
Taught Freshman Composition, 1981-82.

ADMINISTRATIVE EXPERIENCE

Director of Writing Center and Writing Across the Curriculum, Akiba Academy
Planned and revised writing philosophy, curriculum and extracurricular activities; trained faculty in new curriculum and instructional methods (writing across the curriculum); developed resource room and writing labs; revised library skills program; incorporated cooperative learning programs and current literary theories into curriculum; advised students about literary magazine, 1983-89.

English Department Head, Akiba Academy
Interviewed and hired English faculty; supervised and evaluated teachers; implemented new curricula in: literature, study skills, reading, and writing, 1978-82.

Middle States Evaluator, Garnett Valley High School, English Department, Team Head, 1981.

President, Faculty Association, Akiba Academy.
Acted as liaison among faculty, board and administration, 1977-78.

CONSULTING/EDITING EXPERIENCE

Editor of academic and professional manuscripts for publication. Articles appeared in: *Dissociation: Science Teacher*: edited fiction and non-fiction texts, including *Where is Isakjan?* (historical biography).

Consultant to *PCRP II (Pennsylvania Comprehensive Reading Plan)* by Co-author's Name and Co-author's Name, 1989.

PUBLICATIONS

"The Making of Hindsight: Response, Revision, and Teacher Research," in *Understanding Teacher Research*. Ed. Co-editor's Name and Co-Editor's Name. Teachers' College Press (forthcoming, 1991). [Other publications follow.]

WORK IN PROGRESS

Self Presentations in Print: A Guide to Writing College Application Essays.
[Three other listings follow.]

RESEARCH PRESENTATIONS

College Conference on Composition and Communication, Boston: "Talk about Writing and Revision of Rough Drafts," forthcoming.
University of X: "Researching Response," 1989.
Delaware Valley Reading Association and University of X: "Using Protocols to Teach and Research SAT's," 1984.
Ethnography Forum, University of X: "The Organization of Two Groups of Writers," 1984.

FACULTY DEVELOPMENT WORKSHOPS

Invited Speaker, University of X, "In-Process Writing: Moving Toward A First Draft."
[Several other workshops follow.]

ACADEMIC SERVICE

Education Committee
Admissions Committee
Faculty Representative to School Board

PROFESSIONAL/CIVIC MEMBERSHIPS

Lower Merion Committee for a Responsible School Board
Delaware Valley Writing Council
National Council of Teachers of English
Conference on College Composition and Communication

REFERENCES
[Names and addresses of four references follow.]

Sample Vita of Highly Experienced Candidate, Humanities

THOMAS JAMES PROFESSOR

Home Address
Home Phone
Office Phone

EDUCATION

Ph.D., English, University of X, 1981
A.M., English, University of X, 1977
M.A., Education, Stanford University, 1974
A.B., English (Honors), Harvard College, 1972

ACADEMIC EXPERIENCE

Rutgers University, Camden, New Jersey
Associate Professor of English and Director of the Writing Program, 1990-present
Assistant Professor of English and Director of the Writing Program, 1984-90

University of X, Philadelphia, Pennsylvania
Teaching Fellow in English, 1975-78; Lecturer, 1978-79, 1980-84

Chestnut Hill College, Philadelphia, Pennsylvania
Instructor in English, Summer 1978; Instructor (full time), 1979-80

AWARDS

Merit Salary Award, Rutgers University, 1986-87
University Research Council Grants, Rutgers University, 1984-85, 1985-86, 1990-91
Sanderson Prize (Best Essay by a Graduate Student), 1980
Graduate Student Teaching Award, University of X, 1978
Graduated *cum laude* in English, Harvard College, 1972

PUBLICATIONS

Book

Joyce and Wagner: A Study of Influence. Manuscript of 110,000 words, including a fifty-page appendix and a bibliography of 380 items. Forthcoming from Cambridge University Press (Summer 1991).

Essays

"The Voice from the Prompt Box: Otto Luening Remembers James Joyce in Zurich." Co-author's Name. Typescript of twenty-two pages. Forthcoming in *Journal of Modern Literature* (Spring 1991).

"Joyce, Wagner, and the Wandering Jew." *Comparative Literature* 42 (Winter 1990): 49-72.

"Joyce in Philadelphia: An Eyewitless Account." *James Joyce Quarterly* 27 (Winter 1990): 399-406.

"Joyce and Wagner's Pale Vampire." *James Joyce Quarterly* 23 (Summer 1986): 491-96.

Thomas James Professor, 2

"Joyce, Wagner, and the Artist-Hero." *Journal of Modern Literature* 11 (March 1984): 66-88.

"Wagner's *Tannhäuser* in *Exiles*: A Further Source." *James Joyce Quarterly* 19 (Fall 1981): 73-76.

"Henry James and Percy Lubbock: From Mimesis to Formalism." *Novel* 14 (Fall 1980): 20-29.

"The Art and Rhetoric of Chronology in Faulkner's *Light in August*." *College Literature* 7 (Spring 1980): 125-35.

Reviews

Rev. of *Reauthorizing Joyce*, by Vicki Mahaffey. Forthcoming in *Comparative Literature*.

Rev. of *Joyce's Book of the Dark: Finnegans Wake*, by John Bishop. *Comparative Literature* 42 (Summer 1990): 278-79.

Rev. of *Joyce and Prose: An Exploration of the Language of Ulysses*, by John Porter Houston. *James Joyce Literary Supplement* 4 (Spring 1990): 6.

Rev. of *Assessing the 1984 Ulysses*, ed. C. George Sandulescu and Clive Hart. *Journal of Modern Literature* 14 (Fall-Winter 1987): 339.

In progress

Joyce in Context. Collection of essays developed from the academic program of the 1989 James Joyce Conference in Philadelphia. Co-editor's Name.

CONFERENCE PAPERS AND PANELS: JOYCE

"Stephen Dedalus and the Nightmare of Paris." Twelfth International James Joyce Symposium. Monaco, 11 June 1990.

Chair and Panel Discussant on "Annotating 'Oxen of the Sun': 1440-1591, Part 2." Twelfth International James Joyce Symposium. Monaco, 14 June 1990.

Panel Discussant on "*Finnegans Wake*, Book III: The Secret of Shaun's Success." 1989 James Joyce Conference. Philadelphia, 13 June.

[Eleven listings follow.]

CONFERENCE PAPERS AND PANELS: COMPOSITION

"Advanced Writing and Liberal Learning." 1987 Conference on College Composition and Communication. Atlanta, 21 March.

Chair of "Language Across the Curriculum." 1986 Conference on College Composition and Communication. New Orleans, 14 March.

"Writing Across the Curriculum: A Rationale." Faculty of Chestnut Hill College. Philadelphia, 26 September 1985.

[Three listings follow.]

Thomas James Professor, 3

COLLEGE COURSES TAUGHT

Anglo-Irish Literature
Modern British Poetry
The Rise of the Modern Novel
Major Modern Writers: Joyce, Eliot, Faulkner
Contemporary American Fiction and Culture
Senior Writing (Honors Seminar)
English Composition 101, 102

The Twentieth Century British Novel
Modern Drama
Special Topics in Modern British Literature
The American Novel
Survey of American Poetry
Advanced Expository Writing
Basic Skills in Writing

GRANTS

Pennsylvania Humanities Council, for 1989 James Joyce Conference, $18,052
Pennsylvania Council on the Arts, for 1989 James Joyce Conference, $2,500
Fund for Philadelphia, for 1989 James Joyce Conference, $1,500
University Research Council, Rutgers University, 1984-85, 1985-86, 1990-91.

PROFESSIONAL ACTIVITY

Director, 1989 James Joyce Conference, Philadelphia, 12-16 June
Planned a major annual conference with fifty sessions, 147 presenters, audience of 400. Worked with
the endorsement of the James Joyce Foundation. Recruited a Host Committee and Academic Program
Chair, planned special events, identified appropriate sponsors and sites. Wrote three successful
proposals for competitive grants totaling $22,000 and administered budget of $31,000.

"Measurement of Writing Ability II," Philadelphia, August 1984
Served as faculty consultant for a major research project sponsored by the Educational Testing Service.
Project culminated in publication of Breland, et.al., *Assessing Writing Skill: Research Monograph No. 11.*
New York: College Entrance Examination Board, 1987.

Host Committee, 1985 James Joyce Conference, Philadelphia, 12-16 June
Served as one of a nine-member committee that planned and directed a major annual conference.
Organized publicity and wrote program notes.

ADMINISTRATIVE EXPERIENCE

Director, Writing Program, Rutgers University, Camden, 1984-present
Direct and develop a composition program of seven sequenced courses; place all freshmen and transfer
students in appropriate courses; serve on departmental Curriculum Committee; supervise and advise
teaching assistants; chair Writing Program Committee.

Coordinator, Freshman English Program, University of X, 1981-84
Day-to-day direction of a seminar program of 1700 students; drew rosters of 150 courses and
supervised a staff of seventy-five; served as informal adviser to graduate student teaching fellows; sat
on Freshman English Committee and participated in program planning and evaluation. Responsible to
English Department Chair.

Coordinator, Writing Across the University Program, University of X, 1981-84
Directed a new program to support the teaching of writing across the curriculum and in the residence
system; served on planning and evaluation committee; acted as main contact for department chairs,
participating faculty, and writing program fellows; wrote proposals for internal and external support;
administered the program's Writing Center and supervised graduate student tutorial staff.

Chapter 11
Additional Application Materials

Dissertation Abstract

You may be asked to provide an abstract of your dissertation as part of the initial screening process for a faculty position. Or you may wish to provide it with your application whether or not you are specifically asked for it.

Your abstract should conform to the conventions for your field. It is usually one or two pages long. Within the conventions of your discipline make the abstract, and therefore your dissertation, sound interesting and important. Use the active, rather than the passive, construction whenever possible, and stress findings and conclusions where they exist. Rather than saying, "A possible relationship between x and y was studied," say, for example, "Demographic data indicate that x increased as y declined."

Briefly indicate how your research fits into a broader context to answer the implicit "Why should anyone care?" question which may be asked of any piece of research. Someone who reads your abstract should have a clear idea of what your work entailed and want to ask you more about it. Write, rewrite, and seek critiques from your advisor and others in your department until you're satisfied that the abstract will achieve this effect.

Statement of Research Plans

Like an abstract, this short summary (usually one or two pages) may be requested as part of the application process. At other times, you may choose to include it to strengthen your application. Preparing this document is wonderful practice for interviews (see Chapter 13, "Interviewing"), because employers are keenly interested in what you plan to do in the future. It is not expected that you will have begun to do research beyond your dissertation, only that you will have begun to think about it coherently.

If you plan to publish your dissertation as several articles or turn it into a book, you may mention that fact briefly. Be sure, however, to discuss plans for research that extend beyond your dissertation. If your plans sound simply like extensions of your dissertation, or if you use phrases like, "We do this," then you risk giving the impression that you view yourself as an extension of your advisor's research and that you have not begun to think of yourself as an independent researcher.

Give a brief context for your research interests, including how they fit into work others have done, and then discuss your plan for investigation. It is very important to communicate a sense that your research will follow logically from what you have done and be different, important, and innovative. Describing plans at an appropriate level of generality/specificity may require some rewriting and feedback from faculty members. A research plan so specific that one article could complete it is too limited, but one that includes a whole area of study, for example, "labor economics," is too general.

If this document makes the reader want to ask you further questions, even challenge you, it has done its job admirably, because it has helped make it seem that an interview with you would be lively and interesting. Write as clearly and concisely as you can.

Other Things That Might Be Required

While a dissertation abstract and statement of research plans are the additional documents most commonly requested, you may sometimes be asked to submit other materials. A statement of your teaching philosophy, a syllabus for a course you have taught, or a proposal for a course you would like to teach may be requested. If you are in a visual field, such as fine arts or architecture, a portfolio or slides of your work will always be required. Their preparation is beyond the scope of this discussion, but take them very seriously. Your advisor will be able to provide you with guidelines. Seek out his or her critiques, and ask others for theirs as well.

A Note About the Sample Dissertation Abstracts and Statement of Research Interests Which Follow

The following examples, generously volunteered by real candidates, are provided to give you an idea of what such materials look like. We have not changed them in any respect except to omit the authors' names. Custom in your own field might well dictate that yours should be quite different in style, language, or appearance.

Sample Abstract, Social Science

Abstract

THE PSYCHOLOGICAL WELL-BEING OF ELDERLY JEWS:
A COMPARATIVE ANALYSIS

Roger Researcher

Committee Chair's Name

The purpose of this research was to examine the relation of cultural (including religious and ethnic) background to the way in which older individuals respond to questions contained in scales designed to measure psychological well-being. We expected cultural background to be an important predictor of these responses because cultural background influences expressive style, and we suspected that expressive style is part of what is being measured by these scales. We decided to focus our study on the American-Jewish elderly, who have a very expressive affective style.

We selected the Philadelphia Geriatric Center Morale Scale, the Life Satisfaction Index, and the Bradburn Affect Balance Scales to test our hypotheses. For comparison populations, we selected Italian-American Catholics, Irish-American Catholics, and white Presbyterians. These groups were selected because there is a range of expressive styles among these groups.

The data used were three previously collected data sets: the National Senior Citizens Survey, the Myth and Reality of Aging Survey, and the Need, Cost and Effects of Home Services for the Aged Survey.

Two formal hypotheses were tested. The first hypothesis stated that the psychological well-being of Jewish elderly as measured by a standard scale of psychological well-being would be significantly lower than that of members of the non-Jewish groups. The second hypothesis stated that even when holding the major determinants of psychological well-being constant, Jewish status would continue to be a significant predictor of scores on these scales. The hypotheses were tested using a variety of multivariate statistical techniques.

Both hypotheses were confirmed. In addition, the scores of the Jewish respondents were most like the scores of the Italian respondents and least like the scores of the white Presbyterian respondents. We concluded that cultural background does have a significant effect on the patterns of responses of older people to questions designed to measure their psychological well-being. We further concluded that groups noted for expressive styles of behavior have lower average scores on standard scales of psychological well-being than the scores of groups noted for more stoic styles of behavior.

Sample Abstract, Science/Engineering

Spin Alignment and Resonance Behavior in
the ^{24}Mg + ^{24}Mg System

Author's Name

Advisor's Name

ABSTRACT

We have studied heavy-ion resonance behavior in the ^{24}Mg + ^{24}Mg system using particle-γ and particle-γ-γ angular correlation techniques. These methods have allowed us to determine the single and correlated magnetic substate populations for single and mutual inelastic scattering to the 2^+ state in ^{24}Mg in the region of two strong resonances seen at $E_{c.m.} = 45.70$ and 46.65 MeV[1]. Our measurements were performed using the Holifield Heavy Ion Research Facility Spin Spectrometer, a 4π γ-detector array[2]. Our magnetic substate population and angular distribution data for single and mutual inelastic scattering suggest a spin assignment of $J^\pi = 36^+$ for the resonance seen at $E_{c.m.} = 45.70$ MeV. Also, these data suggest a dominant decay l value of $l = 34\hbar$ for this resonance in both single and mutual inelastic scattering. The resonance spin and decay l values are 2 to 4 units above the grazing angular momenta generated by optical model calculations. We used similar techniques to study the one and two α-transfer reactions ^{24}Mg(^{24}Mg, ^{20}Ne)^{28}Si and ^{24}Mg(^{24}Mg, ^{16}O)^{32}S. These data show that the details of these heavy-ion reactions depend critically upon the angular momentum matching properties of these different heavy-ion systems. Our results also suggest weak decay branches for these resonances to the mass-asymmetric ^{16}O+^{32}S system. We use the Rotating Liquid Drop Model to examine the structure of the composite nucleus ^{48}Cr at high spin and excitation energy. The equilibrium shapes, energy levels and fission barriers obtained from these calculations suggest that the observed resonances correspond to the population of highly deformed, high spin states in the composite nucleus ^{48}Cr.

---

[1] First footnote
[2] Second footnote

Sample Abstract, Science/Engineering

Abstract

Progress Toward the Total Synthesis of Acutiphycin

Sara Smith-Researcher
Advisor's Name

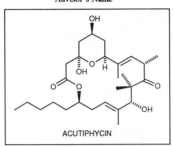

ACUTIPHYCIN

Acutiphycin was isolated in 1984 by Moore and co-workers from the blue-green algae *Osillatoria acutissina*. The macrolide was found to exhibit cytotoxicity and anti-tumor activity.

This dissertation describes in detail synthetic studies directed toward the total synthesis of acutiphycin. Our interest in this macrolide stems from its novel structure and biological activity.

Progress to date includes the construction of several key fragments of the acutiphycin skeleton and the coupling of two key fragments *via* a vinyl anion strategy. Tetrahydropyran 18, available in seven steps from (S)-(-)-malic acid, was elaborated to provide aldehyde 15. To achieve this end, a chelation controlled strategy was used to exploit the stereogenicity present in the tetrahydropyran ring. A stereospecific [2,3] sigmatropic rearrangement then provided ultimately aldehyde 15. A 2-carbon chain homologation, followed by several functional group manipulations then afforded aldehyde 86.

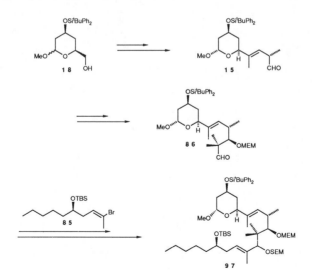

Vinyl bromide **85** was prepared in homochiral form from 1-octene-3-ol. Union of **85** and **86**, followed by the protection of the resulting alcohol, provided **97**, the progenitor to the macrocyclic ring.

Completion of this synthetic venture is envisioned to entail introduction of the remaining 2-carbon unit, followed by macrocyclization, and completion of acutiphycin. As some difficulty was encountered in the addition of a two carbon unit to a derivative of **97**, current efforts are focussed on the construction of aldehyde **106**. Union of **85** and **106** should ultimately afford hydroxy-acid **105**. Macrolactonization, followed by protecting group removal and functional group manipulations will then provide acutiphycin.

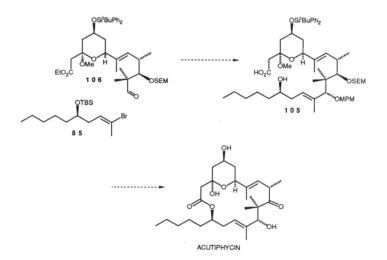

ACUTIPHYCIN

Sample Statement of Research Interests, Humanities

Michelle J. Student

Statement of Research Interests

Current

My dissertation is titled "Popular Deities and Social Change during the Southern Song Period (1127-1270)." Drawing on theory from anthropology of religion, this thesis argues that social change underlay religious change; more specifically, it demonstrates how fluctuations in the relative standing of deities reflected new developments in the lives of their followers. Shifts in the pantheon also heralded the broadening of the cultural and economic spheres of Chinese peasants that occurred in the twelfth and thirteenth centuries. No longer did they worship exclusively local gods. The increasing mobility of cultivators in the lowland, rice-growing regions resulted in their exposure to gods from other places, often to those of merchant groups. Cults in the isolated mountain areas show correspondingly less change.

Studies of Chinese religion usually focus on doctrine, but the absence of sutras and learned monks' debates precludes such an approach to popular religion. Were an anthropologist to ask believers to account for some deities' meteoric ascents and others' equally precipitous descents, they would surely respond that the most powerful deities were the most popular, and the most popular deities, the most powerful. This circular logic meant that one could judge a divinity's strength by the beauty of his image, the opulence of his temple, and the number of government titles he held. What was really going on here? How was it that peasants came to interpret natural events or coincidences as the acts of one specific god? Out of a tangle of dreams, natural events, and chance readings of oracles, a given deity's supporters carded tight, well-reasoned interpretations of divine behavior. Because the attribution of miracles was the product of competition among different groups, records concerning the deities tell us about the lives and thinking of medieval Chinese peasants, a group about whom we know very little.

Future Goals

My first goal is to turn my thesis into a publishable monograph, possibly extending the time period to include the succeeding Yuan (1270-1368) dynasty. While doing my dissertation I have grown increasingly interested in the role of semi-literate groups in Chinese society. Conversant with vernacular Chinese, but uncomfortable in classical Chinese, this stratum acted as brokers between the literati and illiterate. They sometimes wrote inscriptions, but almost never books. Mistaken characters and the use of popular variants in these texts suggest that their grasp of the written language was much less sure than that of the educated. I would like to use the inscriptional collections in China, Japan, and Taiwan as well as published materials to explore a sudden increase in the epigraphic material of the twelfth and thirteenth centuries, which may indicate a possible rise in literacy.

Chapter 12
Cover Letters

Always include a cover letter when you send your vita to an employer. It can serve as a letter of inquiry for determining the staffing needs of a department or as a letter of application for advertised positions. The cover letter is your opportunity to highlight your experience and expertise relevant to the specific institution or position.

Never send out form letters. Address each letter to a specific individual and be sure to use his or her correct title. Sources that list department chairpersons and can probably be found in your campus library are the *Yearbook of Higher Education* and college catalogs. In your letter show some knowledge of the institution and department by examining the course offerings and indicating what you could teach. Check with your advisor to make sure the information is up-to-date. The more information you have about the institution and the position, the better able you will be to write a strong, impressive letter.

It is essential that your letter be well written. How you write, as well as what you say, will be scrutinized carefully. Use simple, direct language and no unnecessary words or sentences. If you are a foreign national and English is not your first language, have a native speaker read your drafts to ensure that the diction sounds natural. Appropriate language may be somewhat less formal than that you would use in your home country. Proofread several times to be sure your spelling and grammar are perfect. Your letter should be printed in a readable typeface. Use a laser or letter-quality printer.

Basic Cover Letter Format

Salutation

Use and spell out the word "professor," e.g., "Dear Professor Smith."

First Paragraph

Explain why you are writing and indicate how you learned about the position, for example, "At the suggestion of Professor Jones . . ."

Middle Paragraph(s)

Highlight your achievements and qualifications, especially those that make you the right person for the position in question. Let the department chair or search committee know what you have to offer without repeating your vita word for word. Relate key items from experience to the specific needs of the organization. Indicate availability for conference interviews. Explain your interest in the institution/position. In general, at a major research institution, it is most important to stress your interest in the department; at a small college, it is also helpful to express an interest in the institution. If you are applying to an institution that stresses teaching and are familiar with and enthusiastic about the kind of students it attracts, say so.

Final Paragraph

Offer to provide extra materials or additional information. Indicate how you can be reached and thank the reader for consideration.

Letters in the humanities tend to be longer (up to two pages) than those in the sciences and social sciences (one page). Have your advisor and others read your early letters to make sure that you are expressing yourself appropriately for your field. If your campus career planning and placement service offers services to doctoral students, counselors there may also be available to critique drafts.

A Note About the Sample Cover Letters Which Follow

The following examples, nearly all generously volunteered by real candidates, are provided to give you an idea of what such letters look like. We have omitted the names of individuals, but have otherwise tried to change the examples as little as possible. They should be regarded as excellent, but not necessarily perfect. As you will see, they vary in style. Write your own letters in a style which is both appropriate to your field and which feels natural to you.

Sample Cover Letter for an Advertised Tenure-Track Position Stressing Teaching

Department Address
Date

Professor Name
English Department, Private College
Address

Dear Professor Name:

I would like to be considered for the tenure-track appointment in American literature announced by your letter to Dr. Name. I am a graduate student finishing my dissertation in English. I expect to complete it by July 1992.

The dissertation traces the development and secularization of the Christian conversion pattern from antiquity through the nineteenth century and examines its use by early twentieth-century American autobiographers. The authors on whom I focus--William and Henry James, Henry Adams, Edith Wharton, Ellen Glasgow, Richard Wright, and Zora Neale Hurston--revise, adapt, and often subvert the socializing function implicit in conversion rhetoric to illustrate their respective roles in a diverse American culture.

My scholarly interests cover a broad range of American topics, including Puritanism, the history of American autobiography, all aspects of nineteenth-century literature and culture, and twentieth-century fiction to the Second World War. I have presented papers on Mark Twain and William James.

I have written articles on the British autobiographical tradition and its relationship to American writing, particularly in a religious context, and, recently the *James Joyce Quarterly* invited me to revise and resubmit my essay on Joyce's use of Renan's Christ. In addition to exposing me to a broad range of American and Old-World literatures, my interest in autobiography has given me a practical knowledge of literary theory and its manifold applications.

The most satisfying of my discoveries during graduate study has been my ability to communicate my enthusiasm for literature to students. For the past five years, I have participated in our freshman seminar program, which combines the studies of literature and composition, and found that combination quite rewarding. Always striving to place the works I teach in a broad cultural context, I have developed courses on the American short story, the American Renaissance, American realism, and American naturalism. I have also taught concentrated composition courses in our Pre-Freshman Program, which invites selected incoming students to participate in an academic and social orientation to university life. Last summer, as well as teaching a section of composition, I was appointed Course Coordinator for the program. For this, I designed, implemented, and administered sixteen sections of English composition.

I will be happy to meet with you, at the MLA Convention or elsewhere, at your convenience. Thank you for your time. I hope to hear from you soon.

Sincerely,

Jean-Paul Student

Sample Cover Letter for an Advertised Tenure-Track Position Stressing Research

Candidate's Address
Date

Professor Name
Professor's Address

Dear Professor Name,

I am writing to apply for the position of Assistant Professor in Hebrew literature beginning fall 1990. Currently I am a doctoral candidate in modern Hebrew and Arabic literatures at the University of X and expect to graduate in May 1990. Two chapters of my dissertation have been completed to date and presented to my department.

My dissertation examines the issues of biculturalism, identity and the mediation of past and present, particularly as they are expressed through language choice. Analyzing the writings of Iraqi-born Israelis within the contexts of exile literature I will explore the factors involved in the choice of language and its effects on thematic and formal aspects of the literature. Paradoxically, those writers with the strongest linguistic competence in Hebrew continue to write in Arabic, while those who came to Israel with less proficiency choose to write in Hebrew. Through textual analysis and the interviews I conducted with the authors themselves, I demonstrate that this choice is more a product of sociopolitical orientation than of linguistic competency. This project not only contributes to the study of Israeli literature but also adds a nonwestern perspective to the study of exile literature and multiculturalism in general.

I have considerable teaching experience both in the United States and abroad in Hebrew and Arabic language and literature. As a graduate student, I was chosen to teach in the "Modern Middle Eastern Literature in Translation" course. This course included works translated from Turkish, Persian, Arabic and Hebrew. I lectured on the genre of poetry and the history of Hebrew literature in addition to leading discussions on Israeli works. I chose specific works to represent significant trends and themes in Israeli literature, and to illustrate different formal aspects of literary discourse and poetics. As a teaching fellow, I was assigned a first-year Hebrew class and full responsibilities for curriculum development, test preparation, proficiency testing, and extracurricular programming. Due to the extremely positive nature of the experience, I am looking for a position that will allow me to teach modern Hebrew language while I continue my interests in Hebrew literature.

In addition to my experience as a teacher, I have also organized a new weekly lecture series for the Oriental Studies Department. While focusing geographically on the Middle East, I invited speakers who presented a wide range of perspectives and topics, such as Afghani narratives, the political crisis in Tunisia, and popular Egyptian music.

I passed the Hebrew University ulpan examination (the 'p'tour') before the start of the academic year (1986-87) and have since maintained my near-native level of oral proficiency as well.

I will be presenting a paper at the Association of Jewish Studies conference in December. I would be pleased to meet with you then, or at any other time that is convenient for you. Please find enclosed a copy of my curriculum vitae. Letters of recommendation will follow under separate cover. If any additional information is requested, please do not hesitate to contact me. Thank you for your consideration.

Sincerely,

Alyssa Candidate

Sample Cover Letter Requesting a Convention Interview

Candidate's Address
Date

Professor Blank
Department of English
Address

Dear Professor Blank:

I am writing in response to your description in the October *MLA Job Information List* of a position as Assistant Professor of English. I am currently completing my dissertation at the University of X under the direction of Dr. Name. Supported by a Mellon Dissertation Fellowship, I will fulfill all Ph.D. requirements by the end of this year.

The dissertation, "Realism at Risk: The Representation of Art in Victorian Fiction," argues that the preoccupation with art in novels by Charlotte Bronte, Thackeray, Eliot, and Hardy is, paradoxically, an articulation of the nineteenth-century movement towards realism. Focusing on individual novels which represent a variety of artistic modes -- the superficial perspective of visual art, the deliberately deceptive world of the theater, and the authentic realm of music -- it traces the process by which this artistic cross-referencing allows the different arts to denote varying degrees of truth. I suggest that while these novelists endanger their own claim to "truth" by insisting on the illusiveness of art, in fact the effect of openly invoking the problem of representation is ultimately to defuse it. Bronte and Thackeray link all arts with artifice in a way which allows their own novels to stand outside the structures of deception framed within their texts. Eliot and Hardy go a step further to develop a hierarchy of artistic metaphors which functions as a complex representational code. This delineation of multiple levels of representation helps the novelists to construct densely realistic fictional worlds.

My article "'The Language of the Soul': George Eliot and Music," forthcoming in *Nineteenth-Century Literature*, examines Eliot's exploitation of the ambiguous cultural status of music in the nineteenth century. Although the dissertation focuses on Victorian literature, my interest in interdisciplinary studies extends from the Romantic period to the twentieth century. This fall, I will have the opportunity to present a paper on music in Wordsworth and Radcliffe at the Mid-Hudson MLA Conference, and later this year I will present a paper on musical films at the Northeast Modern Language Association (NEMLA) Conference.

The Dean's Award for Distinguished Teaching which I received suggests the extent of my commitment to exploring literature in the classroom as well as in the library. As a graduate student I have had the freedom to design and teach my own freshman seminars on subjects ranging from the Victorian novel to modern poetry. The two courses I developed which deal with fictions of revision reflect my interest in the tension created by one art object's reference to another; by pairing modern writers with their literary predecessors (for example, Jean Rhys and Charlotte Bronte, Margaret Drabble and George Eliot, Tom Stoppard and Shakespeare), I encouraged my students to see literature as a response to the multiple ways, both real and fictional, of constructing the world.

I would be glad to meet with you for an interview at the December MLA Convention or elsewhere at your convenience. I can be reached at the above address and telephone number until December 22, after which I can be reached at [phone, address]. Thank you for your consideration. I look forward to hearing from you.

Sincerely yours,

Jamie Graduate

Sample Cover Letter in Response to an Expression of Interest

Department Address
Date

Professor Name
Recruiting Chair
Department of Political Science
Large University
Address

Dear Professor Name:

My dissertation chair, Dr. Name, indicated that you are interested in reviewing my qualifications for the Assistant Professor position in your department. I would like to be considered for this position and am therefore sending you my curriculum vitae and an abstract of my dissertation, "The Electronic Town Meeting: Impacts of Polling on Local Party Nominations." I particularly appreciate your interest because the work of several of your faculty members has been important in my own research.

I plan to attend the American Political Science Association meetings in August. I would be glad to meet with you or your colleagues then. As it happens, I will be in California two weeks from now, and, if it is convenient for you, would also be glad to schedule a meeting with you then.

Thank you for your interest and consideration.

Sincerely,

Ahmed Q. Student

Sample Cover Letter for a One-Year Appointment

Address
Date

Dr. Name
Chair
Department of Philosophy and Religion
Address

Dear Dr. Name:

I would like to be considered for the one-year replacement position in the Department of Philosophy and Religion, as advertised in the January 10, 1991, issue of *The Chronicle of Higher Education*. I am a doctoral candidate (ABD) in Ancient History at the University of X. My major field of study is Assyriology, and my minor field is biblical history and literature.

Your advertisement mentions a General Education course on the origins of Western Civilization. My academic background, teaching interests and experiences have dwelt on the the first 3,000 years of civilization (beginning a little before the invention of writing in Sumer). I have read, in cuneiform, significant parts of such great, ancient literary works as the Gilgamesh Epic and Enuma Elish, and of course I am familiar with the Hebrew Bible. The course which I taught at Syracuse University College ("A Dozen of the World's Firsts: History Began at Sumer") utilized this knowledge and additional facets of life at that time, such as architecture, mathematics, and recipes. Comments (written anonymously) from course participants mentioned my knowledge, enthusiasm, and humor as its most positive aspects. I have also taught Bible History for three years at a private, college-preparatory high school.

I have had coursework in the ancient history of Anatolia, Syro-Palestine, Egypt, and Greece. At Princeton Seminary, I had several courses on the history and structure of the biblical text, including a year of Greek. Last fall, to update my knowledge of later periods of Western Civilization, I sat in on a course on the Renaissance, at Syracuse University.

With respect to the course you describe, "Introduction to Religion," I regard my seminary education and my life experience as an excellent place from which to study, analyze, and compare other belief systems (and I know that extensive library in Chapel House!). My years of work on the Arab-Israeli conflict have given me not only an intellectual but also a "visceral" understanding of the various styles of belief (and non-belief) in modern Judaism and Islam.

I note that you do not specifically request letters of recommendation or transcripts. Should you desire any of these or copies of my published articles, please do not hesitate to contact me at [phone number]. Thank you for your consideration. I look forward to hearing from you.

Sincerely,

Alice Applicant

Sample Letter of Inquiry When No Position Is Advertised

Candidate's Address
Date

Dean Name
College of Architecture
University of Z
Address

Dear Dean Name,

I am completing my doctoral degree in architecture at the University of X, Graduate School of Fine Arts. My focus is on the field of Architectural Technology, which has been a strong interest since my master's study at M.I.T., where my major was in Building Systems. This interest is also reflected in my dissertation, "Buildings as Cyborgs: Expressions of Hand and Machine Craftsmanship in Architecture." I am seeking a full-time teaching position in architecture commencing this fall.

Both my teaching and research focus on bridging the gap between the making and the made in architecture, through a conscientious integration of theory and practice. As I understand this goal is shared by many of your faculty, I believe I could be an active participant in the school.

I am enclosing a copy of my curriculum vitae and reference list for your review and consideration. If you would like to see my portfolio or any other materials, please do not hesitate to contact me at the above address.

I look forward to hearing from you soon. Thank you for your consideration.

Sincerely,

Mehri Aspirant

Part IV
Conducting the Search

Chapter 13
Interviewing

The academic interviewing process may encompass two different types of events: the short half-hour to hour-long screening interview at an annual conference or convention which serves as the central job clearinghouse for a field, and the all-day interview on campus which may follow a successful conference interview. If you are invited to interview for a job as a result of your direct response to an advertisement, an all-day campus interview may well be the first, and only, stage in the interviewing process.

While there are many similarities between kinds of interviews, each presents its own challenges. At a conference interview you have a very limited amount of time to stand out in a field of candidates, often under rushed and stressful conditions. In this setting you need to be prepared to present your qualifications succinctly and interestingly. An all-day campus visit is a far more complex event. It usually requires a presentation and involves more people, a greater variety of social situations, and more ambiguity.

Any sort of interview, however, is far more like ordinary professional conversations than different from them. Any time two people meet each other, they form an impression of each other. An interview differs only in that the evaluative dimension is more explicit. Whenever you encounter an unanticipated situation, do what you would ordinarily do in a professional setting, and it is likely that your impulse will be correct.

In ordinary conversation, if you are asked a question you do not understand, you ask for clarification, rather than panic. If you say something that produces a puzzled expression on your listener's face, you ask if there is something you can clarify. If a question spontaneously occurs to you as a result of something the other person has said, you ask it. If you can't answer a question, you say so. All these responses are appropriate in an interview. Most interviewers are far more impressed by candidates who appear confident and candid than by those who appear to be trying to give the "right" answers. While you should always give the interviewer the opportunity to take the lead, many people who conduct interviews are far more comfortable if the candidate feels free to volunteer information and ask questions.

Areas You Will Need to Discuss

In any interview for a faculty position, be prepared to address these concerns: your dissertation, your teaching, your future research plans, and your interest in the organization to which you are applying.

Your Dissertation

Be prepared to explain your work to the variety of people you may encounter in an interview, from world experts in your area of specialization through the person outside the department, such as a dean, whose work may have been in another discipline entirely. Practice particularly the way you will explain your work to those totally unfamiliar with its context. The effort you will need to make to be concise and to explain relevance in that case may well also improve your more technical presentation to experts in the field.

You could discuss your work for hours, but prepare to begin with a brief summary (about a paragraph long). It should leave the interviewer with the impression that he or she knows what you did (be clear); the work was interesting (speak with enthusiasm, and mention interesting findings or conclusions early in your discussion); the work was important (discuss how your work relates to other work and suggest areas for future exploration). Once you've captured this level of interest, further discussion becomes much easier.

Your Future Research Interests

It's imperative that you appear to have some! Merely saying that you plan to publish your dissertation isn't enough. You may be so immersed in it that it's hard to look beyond its completion. If so, set time aside to think about what you might do next. The effort will be worth your time. A candidate who says, "I haven't thought about that yet," when asked about research plans places himself or herself at an enormous disadvantage.

Prepare to discuss your ideas at a convincing level of detail. If you will require external funding to do your research, be aware of probable funding sources. Try to convey enough enthusiasm about your ideas that you will carry your audience along with your enthusiasm and interest.

Teaching

A hiring department's interest in this topic will vary, but most will have at least some degree of interest in what you do in front of a class. Be prepared to discuss your approach to teaching, successful teaching experiences you have had, and new courses you would be prepared to offer. When you discuss a course, be able to suggest the text you might use. It is helpful to find out in advance what is currently in use in the department. Even if you would not plan to use the same text, it is neither necessary nor wise to disparage the current choice. Don't forget that junior faculty members are often expected to carry a great deal of the introductory teaching load. If this isn't your great joy in life, you needn't pretend that it is, but try to convey the impression that you will do introductory teaching competently and with good humor.

Your Interest in the Institution

Major research universities may consider it obvious that you would like to work for them, and a small liberal arts college in a remote location may press you more on the topic of why you want the job. But your enthusiasm for the department and the job is always important. After all, the people who are interviewing you work there, and it is not flattering to them if you seem to find their jobs uninteresting. You usually need to convey interest most strongly at less prestigious universities and at four-year colleges of all descriptions. The latter tend to pride themselves on distinctive institutional personalities and to hire people whom they believe will fit in.

Research the department before the interview. When you are invited, it is appropriate to ask the person who calls you to send you materials that would give you information about the department and school. Read catalogs and college guides to learn about the school. The informal guides to college written for high school seniors are particularly useful in conveying the atmosphere of an institution. Use library indices and data bases to learn about the research of faculty members. Use word of mouth to find out how others view the school.

In general, departments are looking, not only for a candidate with outstanding independent research potential, but also for an outstanding colleague who will enrich the department, not simply by being present, but also by interacting productively with others. Nothing flatters a faculty member more than having a candidate talk knowledgeably about how interesting the faculty member's research is. Try to search out and explore in advance areas of potential collaboration with faculty in the department.

During the interview, you do not need to be insincere to convey enthusiasm. Just talk about what you do find attractive about the institution. If there are no reasons at all that it appeals to you, why are you interviewing there?

Illegal Interview Questions

It may be helpful to you to know that employers cannot lawfully ask you questions that lead to illegal discrimination on the basis of race, sex, religion, national origin, or physical disability. However, as many candidates have found, the fact that questions are potentially illegal does not mean that they may not be asked. Try to respond to such questions calmly, answering the concerns they raise without necessarily volunteering the information they request:

Question: Do you plan to have children?
Answer: I see that you're concerned about my commitment to this position. Let me tell you about my research plans for the next several years. I plan to pursue them, whatever other personal decisions I may make.

Question: Did you grow up speaking Spanish?
Answer: Are you interested in hiring a native speaker for this position?

Some illegal questions are asked out of ignorance; others are a mistaken way to get information about one issue by asking about another (a common example is asking about a spouse's job in order to determine how long you are likely to stay in a position). Try not to react to them confrontationally and to use them as another way to demonstrate your professionalism. Feel free, however, not to provide information that you cannot legally be asked to give.

Question: What does your spouse do?
Answer: (If you feel that providing the information might work to your advantage.) We're fortunate that he's a systems consultant, and can work anywhere he has a telephone line.

If you are very uncomfortable with the direction a question is taking, you may politely ask the interviewer why that question is important and how it relates to the position you are seeking. This should alert the interviewer that you feel the question is inappropriate. Be aware, however, that there is some risk associated with this approach:

Question: Are you married?
Answer: Can you tell me how you feel that that would be impor-
                  tant for the position we're discussing?

Sometimes it is to your advantage to volunteer information that your interviewers may hesitate to request. The law can regulate what is viewed as appropriate to ask, but it does not eliminate employers' concerns, whether they are legitimate or not. For example, if you have a physical disability, your interviewers may appreciate it if you explain how you work with it. If you are much older than the average job candidate, it may be helpful to volunteer remarks that will give the impression that you can work comfortably with younger colleagues. If you are visibly pregnant, you may choose to make direct reference to the sincerity of your interest in the job. Be alert to comments that may reveal a concern.

Comment: We were all impressed by the years you had spent in
                   business before you got your Ph.D.
Response: Yes, I really enjoyed those years. I feel fortunate to have
                   the opportunity to prove myself again in a new field.
                   (Indirectly addresses concern that age and experience
                   may make him or her unable to work comfortably in a
                   junior position.)

A Note About Attire

Wear something that conveys a professional appearance and won't detract attention from what you have to say. In general, this means for men a suit or pants and a jacket, and for women a dress, suit, or skirt with jacket. Dress more casually for informal events which may be planned as part of an all-day visit. For example, watch what is worn by candidates who are interviewing with your own department. Quality and professionalism are more important than variety. Invest in one good outfit and use changes of shirts or accessories to avoid being a re-run of yourself from one day to the next. Have a portfolio or briefcase, even if it is an inexpensive one, to keep track of papers and handouts.

When All Else Fails

It happens to nearly everyone. Nervousness about how you are doing in an interview interferes with showing yourself at your best. This is why some people actually interview better with departments they are less interested in. Your preparation for the interview should include enough sleep or exercise or whatever else lets you approach it in as relaxed a fashion as possible.

If you pay too much attention to "body language" during an interview, you will probably distract yourself from the points you are trying to address. However, be aware of how you tend to show nervousness (tapping feet, clasping hands, or whatever) and during the interview occasionally notice how you are behaving. If you are not sitting in a fairly open, relaxed position, change to one. Sitting with your arms crossed or holding your hands creates a closed, uncomfortable impression, and sitting more confidently will probably make you feel more confident as well. Holding your breath is a common nervous reaction that makes your speech choppy. Remember to breathe as you speak, and you will appear more relaxed.

Learn to use introductory "structuring" phrases which will let you buy time before trying to answer a question that throws you. They are better than twisting your hands or saying "um." For example:

- That's an interesting question. Let me take a moment to decide how best to respond to it.
- We need to consider several factors. First . . .
- I've never considered it from that point of view, but perhaps . . .
- I'd be glad to tell you about it.
- I'm sorry, but I'm not sure I understand your question. Do you mean . . .

You are expected to be somewhat nervous, but if you feel nervousness is getting in the way of expressing yourself clearly or is making your interviewers uncomfortable, it is best to make a direct reference to it. Paradoxically, the minute you admit you are nervous, you are likely to become less so, as well as to relax the interviewer. Examples of "defusing" statements might be:

- Excuse me for speaking so rapidly. I've been looking forward to the chance to speak with you.
- Excuse me, but let me take a second to collect my thoughts. I'm a little nervous, because I'm so interested in this opportunity.
- Let me begin this explanation again. I can see that I didn't express myself clearly.

Preparation

Advance preparation, of course, will let you approach interviews with less nervousness and even with some enjoyment. The end of this chapter includes a list of typical questions. The chapters on "Conference and Convention Interviews" and "Campus Interviews" have checklists for these interview situations.

While you certainly don't want to memorize your responses word for word, it is helpful before any interview to fix in your mind the main points you would like to make, given the probable interests of the employer. Prepared with the knowledge of what you wish to discuss, you can use even unexpected questions that come your way as an opportunity to discuss the ideas that you wish to convey.

Many departments or campus career planning and placement offices offer practice interview sessions. If yours does, plan to take advantage of the sessions. If it doesn't, try to organize one. Ask a faculty member to give you an individual interview. If you have access to videotape equipment, taping an interview will give you the clearest possible idea of how you will come across. If you don't have access to video, you can still get a good idea of your responses by making an audio tape.

In addition, departments provide an excellent forum for delivering the presentation you plan to give at a campus interview. Take advantage of this opportunity, welcome feedback, and add final polish to your interview presentation.

Questions That Might Be Asked in an Academic Interview

About Research

* Why did you choose your dissertation topic?
* Can you tell us briefly what theoretical framework you used in developing your research?
* Of course you've read _____? (names an unfamiliar article/book related to your dissertation).
* If you were to begin it again, are there any changes you would make in your dissertation?
* In doing your research, why didn't you _____? (This question can take many forms. You are being asked to respond appropriately to an intellectual challenge to your work.)

- What contribution does your dissertation make to the field? Is it important?
- You realize that several members of this department tend to approach the subject from a very different perspective than does your advisor . . .
- Tell me about your dissertation (asked in a meeting with a dean who knows very little about your field).
- Why didn't you finish your dissertation sooner?
- I see you have very few publications . . .
- What are your research plans for the next two/five/ten years?
- What are your plans for applying for external funding over the next few years?
- What facilities do you need to carry out your research plans?
- Do you plan to apply for any major funding?

About Teaching

- Are you a good teacher?
- How do you feel about having to teach required courses?
- What is your approach to teaching introductory _____?
- How do you motivate students?
- How would you encourage students to major in our field?
- In your first semester you would be responsible for our course in _____. How would you structure it? What textbook would you use?
- Many of our students are probably (more/less academically talented; older/younger) than those you've become used to at your institution. How successful would you be with them?
- What is your teaching philosophy?
- If you could teach any course you wanted to, what would it be?
- Have you had any experience with the case study method?
- What do you think is the proper relationship between classroom instruction and professional exposure?

About Your Willingness to Participate in the Department and School

- Can you summarize the contribution you would make to our department?
- Are you willing to become involved in committee work?
- Why are you interested in our kind of school?
- What institutional issues particularly interest you?

About Your Career and Personal Choices

- If you have more than one job offer, how will you decide?
- How do you feel about living in a small college town like this in an isolated rural area?
- I can't imagine why a young person like you would want to go into this field . . .
- I understand your spouse is completing his/her Ph.D. What if you receive job offers in different locations? (This question is not legal in most contexts, but you should be prepared for it.)
- What do you do in your spare time?
- Who else is interviewing you?
- What will it take to persuade you to take this job?
- What kind of salary are you looking for?

Do You Have Any Questions for Us?

The right answer to this is always yes, or you risk appearing uninterested. Prepare some questions in advance, but, above all, ask questions that show a response to what you have learned from the interviewers, and that are lively, rather than formulaic.

Questions about salary and benefits are not appropriate now. Wait until you are offered a job to ask about these matters.

Chapter 14
Conference and Convention Interviews

Challenges of the Conference or Convention Interview

Conference interviews may be relatively unimportant in your field. In other disciplines, however, preliminary interviews for most of the entry-level jobs in the country may be held at the annual meeting. You may be one of ten or more well-qualified candidates on a long interview schedule, interviewing under conditions of stress and possible confusion. So what do you do? First, reassure yourself that other job candidates face the same situation. Practice before the convention so that you can convey key information succinctly and make the most of limited time. Practice ensures that when the interview arrives you can relax and respond flexibly to interviewers, knowing that you're prepared for whatever arises.

Be prepared to be interviewed by a group. Three to six department members is a typical size, but it is possible that the number might be much larger. When you schedule your interview, ask the person who is arranging it how many people will probably interview you, so that you have some idea of what to expect. You may have interviews in hotel public areas set aside for that purpose. Some departments will have taken suites of rooms for interviewing. Others will interview in an ordinary hotel bedroom.

While you may be happy to interview with everyone who wants to talk to you, be realistic in scheduling interviews. Allow enough time to get from one location to another, bearing in mind that interviews may run behind schedule. Don't book yourself so tightly that you arrive late and disheveled to speak with the institution that is your first choice.

Keeping Your Audience

Important as the job interview is to you, it may be less interesting to members of the interviewing team. They may be preoccupied with other aspects of the conference, be tired, and find that interviewing a long series of candidates is not their preferred occupation. Make every effort not to bore them! You are very likely to be asked to discuss your dissertation. Try hard to give a succinct introduction to your subject and to gauge your audience's immediate reaction, adding more or less detail as their responses suggest.

During each interview, try to introduce something that will make you memorable. This could be some striking aspect of your research, the fact that your advisor used to be a member of this department, the fact that you're tri-lingual, or anything else that will help people remember who you are. Even if one member of a group does nearly all the talking, address your responses to everyone and try to make eye contact with everyone in the room.

Dealing with Difficult Situations

At a convention you may encounter other situations that do not conform to a script for the perfect interview. There may be schedule confusion, department members may float in and out of the interview suite, or an interviewer may have had too much to drink. Anything you can do to appear unruffled will work to your advantage. Try not to let annoyance at an interviewer's behavior get the best of you.

Always feel free to act in a way that maintains your sense of personal dignity. If anything inappropriate occurs (for example, if an interviewer keeps pressing you to have a drink when you don't want one), realize that setting personal limits is appropriate and will serve you well in the long run: "Thanks, no. I'd like to begin to discuss the position you advertised."

In the extremely unlikely event that you find yourself in what you regard as an impossible interview, in which all your best efforts do not dissuade the interviewer from creating a humiliating situation, feel free to terminate the interview, as calmly as you can: "I'd like to discuss the position, but now doesn't seem to be a good time," or, "There doesn't seem to be a good match between our interests, so I won't take more of your time. Thanks for inviting me to the interview." In such a case check immediately with your advisor or someone else from your department who is attending the conference. If anything seriously inappropriate has occurred, it may be possible to arrange another interview under better conditions.

Usually, however, convention interviews are hectic but professional. Try not to get annoyed at minor issues and to keep a sense of humor. Everyone else will be interviewing under the same stressful conditions, and things won't go perfectly for anyone.

A Desirable Dilemma: Early Offers

Recently, in fields in high demand, candidates have been receiving immediate invitations to campus interviews, or even job offers, as a result of convention interviewing. While most candidates long for just this sort of dilemma, and the attention can be flattering, try to keep a sense of perspective. You may feel you have little to lose by accepting another campus visit, but stop short of exhausting yourself by making numerous trips to places where you have no interest in working.

If you receive an offer before you feel you have had a reasonable chance to explore the market, express pleasure at having received it, but explain that you need more time to make up your mind, and negotiate for as long as you can before you need to make a final decision. Don't let the overtures affect your perspective to such an extent that you begin to seem arrogant, an attitude that can quickly alienate even those who were initially very enthusiastic about your candidacy.

Conference or Convention Interview Checklist

Before the Interview

Get all the details straight when you arrange for the interview:

- How interviews are arranged varies from convention to convention. Find out from your own department how yours works.
- Clarify the time and place for each interview. If possible, find out how many people will interview you and learn their names.
- If interviews will be held at more than one hotel, make sure that you know how you will get from one to another, and how long it will take, so that your schedule is realistic. Seek help from your department here.
- If there is enough time before the interview, ask to have sent to you any materials that would help you learn more about the school and department.
- Make sure you have the name and phone number of the contact person in case you need to reach him or her before the meeting.

Learn about the institution, departments, and interviewers:

- You may have limited time for research, especially if you have many interviews scheduled. In the time available, try to learn something about every school and become fairly knowledgeable about the ones that interest you most.
- Use catalogs. The many readily available college guides written for high school seniors will give you a quick profile of the institution.
- Use databases and manual searches for information on publications by department members.
- Ask everyone who might know something about the institution to discuss it.
- Learn whether the department stresses teaching or research.

Prepare for the interview:

- Decide what you want to convey.
- Practice answering questions with a friend, a faculty member, or a career planning and placement counselor.

Bring:

- Extra copies of your vita.
- Copies of your dissertation abstract and statement of research plans.
- Other materials you may wish to show, if time permits: syllabi, reprints, abstracts of articles. You will not necessarily distribute all of these, but you will be prepared with them should you need them.
- Whatever accessories or repair materials (buttons, glasses, or an extra pair of contact lenses) you might need, to avoid last-minute sartorial disasters.
- Don't check anything important through on the airplane. Bring all the essentials in carry-on luggage.

During the Interview

- If possible, begin by shaking hands with the interviewer(s), even if you need to take the initiative to do so.
- If schedule problems cause you to arrive late for an interview, apologize, and then try to forget it and begin on a calm note.
- If you don't catch a name when you're introduced to someone, have it repeated, so that you know it.

- Do your best, and concentrate on the conversation with the interviewers and the ideas you are trying to convey, rather than on how well you are "performing."
- When your interview ends, briefly summarize your interest in the position and what you feel you could contribute to it. Keep it short.
- If possible, shake hands with the interviewer(s) when you leave.

After the Interview

It is not necessary to write a thank-you note unless the interviewers have done something special, such as taking you out for a meal.

Chapter 15
Campus Interviews

Challenges of the Campus Visit

By the time a department invites three to five candidates for an all-day visit, it has probably determined that all are in some sense competent. During the interview day the search committee tries to assess such intangibles as "potential," "fit," and "tenurability." On campus, it is as important to be prepared to be convincing and concise as it is at a conference. In addition, the abilities to respond flexibly to the requirements of unpredictable situations, to talk comfortably with others in informal, unstructured meetings, and to convey interest in the institution to which you're applying will help you land the job.

A day and evening on campus conceivably could involve a presentation to faculty, a lecture to a class, a group interview, several individual meetings, some meals, and a reception. You may meet individuals ranging from a dean to a junior representing the departmental majors' club, from genuinely stimulating potential colleagues to the curmudgeon who makes it his or her business to ask any speakers to relate their presentations to the curmudgeon's own field of thirty-year-old research. Flexibility and a sense of humor will serve you well. Be prepared for potentially problematic aspects of the day-long visit.

The Presentation and Its Question Session

The importance of an excellent seminar can hardly be overemphasized. An outstanding seminar can make up for many other shortcomings, but a poor seminar is seldom forgiven. The seminar is used as an opportunity to see what the candidate has done in terms of research; how he or she handles questions and thinks on his or her feet; how he or she performs in the classroom; and even whether he or she has a sense of humor and a stage presence that suggest he or she will be successful at conferences, in the classroom, and in other professional forums.

In the question period following a presentation, you may receive questions that leave you at a loss, that point to a weakness in your work, or that are challenging to the point of hostility. Stay calm and don't let yourself be put on the defensive. Be confident enough to admit that you don't know something. Respond to even unreasonable questions reasonably. Be prepared to venture reasonable hypotheses. Practice in advance how you might respond to even the most off-the-wall questions about your presentation.

The Broken-Record Syndrome

You may meet many people throughout the day without having a very clear idea of who is critical to the decision to hire you. Simultaneously you may begin to tire of hearing yourself discuss the same subjects over and over. It's extremely important that you be enthusiastic about these topics with each new person that you meet. Everyone who meets you will want to form his or her own impression of you. So tell your story again to each new person with as much zest and interest as if it were for the first time.

The Social Event

Social occasions are usually part of a day-long visit. Realize that they are also part of the screening process. Follow your hosts' lead in deciding how much to talk shop and how much to talk about topics of general interest. It is a good idea, however, to seize every reasonable opportunity to discuss your work and your field. You can also appropriately ask questions during these times. Your host will appreciate it if you make yourself good company: ask questions of others; initiate conversation; laugh at other people's jokes; and display an interest in the people you are with.

If you have no personal objection to doing so, drink if others do, but don't drink enough to affect your behavior. Alcohol and interviewing can be a risky combination. One compromise is to have a glass of what is offered but to drink only part of it. Particularly beware of "confessional" impulses. However friendly your hosts, do not confide that you are here just for practice, that you can't wait to put distance between yourself and your advisor, or any other statement that later you are almost sure to regret having made.

It is easier to handle these occasions if you are very outgoing than if you are shy, but shy people can convey their interest and intelligence through active questioning and perceptive listening. But you must push yourself to be an active participant in the occasion. It is better to risk some less-than-perfect remarks and come across as an individual than as a quiet, inoffensive presence, so bland that no one is sure what you are like or what you really think.

Your Opportunity to Learn About the Institution

Interviewing is a two-way process. Even as others are assessing your candidacy for the position, you have an opportunity to learn about the institution and to decide whether or not you want to work there. Both schools and departments have their own institutional cultures. You are most likely to thrive in a department and school in which there is a reasonable measure of fit between you and the others who work and study there. Take advantage of your time on campus to learn everything you can.

Location and Physical Setting

Gauge your own reaction to the appearance of the campus. Does it strike you as lively and inviting? Or do you feel that it is impersonal? In the middle of nowhere? Impossibly urban and congested? It's unlikely that you would choose a job entirely based on its physical setting and appearance, but it is important to be able to visualize yourself as at least reasonably comfortable going to work there every day. Look carefully at the physical plant itself, particularly the part of it where you would be working. Do offices and research facilities appear adequate? If laboratory or computer facilities are particularly important in your work, your hosts will be likely to give you a tour or demonstration of them. If not, however, and such facilities are important to you, ask.

The Department

Probably the single most important thing you will learn on a campus visit is what the members of the department are like. These are the people with whom you will interact on a daily basis, who will be available for discussion of ideas, and who will ultimately evaluate your performance. Will you be glad to be part of this group? It is certainly important to keep an open mind and to remember that first impressions are necessarily somewhat superficial. Nevertheless, your "irrational" reactions to these individuals are some of the most important data you can gather during your visit.

Pay attention to how people appear to react to each other. Does the

departmental atmosphere appear lively and collegial? Extremely hierarchical? Are there obvious divisions between competing factions? Do
people appear enthusiastic about where they are and what they are
doing, or is there a pervasive sense of cynicism and discouragement?

Students

If you are particularly interested in teaching and your visit does not
include any planned meetings with students, ask faculty members to
describe both students and classes. If your visit includes any free time,
you may want to spend it at the student union or other campus gathering place. Listen to what students say to each other. Introduce yourself
and ask them questions. Pick up copies of the student paper and of any
other student-produced publications. They will give you a feel for
current campus issues.

The Broader Institution

At a university, probably you will feel you work in your department and
your school more than in the institution as a whole. At a college you will
probably feel that the college itself is your employer. When you visit,
you will probably spend at least some time with someone who repre-
sents a unit larger than your prospective department. Use this as an
opportunity to evaluate the role that the department plays in the
broader picture. Is it strong and respected? Slowly eroding? The
bright, brash new kid on the block?

   As you learn throughout the day, feel free to comment positively on
what you are learning. For example, if your first interview of the day is
with someone who devotes a great deal of time to describing the
school's excellent computer resources, in the next interview you can
explain that you were impressed with them and go on to explain why
these facilities would be particularly advantageous in your own research. If you notice an extremely collegial atmosphere throughout
the day, and at the end of the day the chair asks what you think of the
department, by all means say that you've observed a lively exchange of
ideas and are very attracted by that kind of atmosphere. Hiring committees like to know that you have read their institution correctly and
can picture yourself functioning well in it.

On-Campus Interview Checklist

Before the Interview

Get all the details straight when you arrange for the interview:

- Find out the length of the interview day and what meetings to expect during it.
- Will you be making a presentation? If so, on what? how long? to whom? how should it be delivered?
- Will you be expected to teach a class? If so, to whom? on what?
- Confirm all travel arrangements. Find out how they should be booked. Save all receipts. Allow more than enough time to compensate for flight delays or traffic jams.
- Make sure you know the name of the person who has called you, where you are to arrive, how you will be met, the name of the person who will meet you, and all relevant phone numbers.
- If there is enough time before the interview, ask to have any materials that would help you learn more about the school and department sent to you.
- If you encounter unavoidable delays while traveling to the interview, call as soon as you can and explain why you will be delayed.

Learn about the institution and faculty:

- Use catalogs.
- Use database and manual searches for information on publications by members of the department. Try to learn the names of everyone in the department, so you can address them by name during your visit.
- Ask everyone who might know something about the institution to discuss it.

Practice:

- Practice your presentation.
- Time your talk to ensure it's the right length.
- Practice a "cocktail party length" brief summary to give to those outside the department.
- Be sure your transparencies or handouts are ready in plenty of time.

Bring:

- Extra copies of your vita.
- Copies of your dissertation abstract.
- Copies of your statement of research interests.
- More than enough handouts. Make sure they look good.
- Samples of syllabi for courses you designed, reprints, abstracts of articles. You will not necessarily distribute all of these during the day but you'll be prepared with them if you need them.

- Something to do during delays in traveling.
- Whatever you need (running clothes, bubble bath, escapist novels) if you'll be nervous the night before the interview.
- Don't check anything important through on the airplane. Bring all the essentials in carry-on luggage.

During the Interview

- Remember that each new person you meet hasn't heard your story yet. Be prepared to tell it again and again with enthusiasm.
- If the day includes social events, follow your hosts' leads in deciding how much to talk about professional, and how much about social, topics.
- If you don't catch a name when you're introduced to someone, have it repeated, so that you know it. Shake hands when you meet someone.
- Acknowledge everyone present in a group interview, and, if possible, say goodbye to people individually when you leave.
- At the end of the day, find out when a decision will be made, and when you may call if you haven't heard anything.
- Find out if you should turn in receipts then, or send them later.

After the Interview

- Take care of any extra receipts.
- Write a thank-you note to the main person who arranged your day. You can ask that person to convey your thanks to others. Reiterate your interest in the position. It isn't necessary to write to everyone with whom you spoke.

Chapter 16
Job Offers, Negotiations, and Acceptances

Having produced written materials, identified job openings, applied for positions, and interviewed at conventions and on-campus, you anticipate the time when, after all your effort, you get a job offer, or possibly several. Keep your job search as active as possible until you receive at least one offer that appeals to you. Once an offer is made, you may have to agree on a timetable for acceptance, decide on your first choice, negotiate with a first choice school when you have to meet a deadline for accepting another offer, negotiate salary or working conditions, and deal appropriately with schools that you accept and reject.

First, make sure that you really do have an offer. The department member who tells you confidentially that you're the committee's first choice or the chairman who says that the department is virtually certain that funds will be approved are not offering positions, merely expressing optimism. A job offer becomes a real offer when a salary and term of appointment are attached to it and when someone has put it in writing. If you turn down a job in which a letter offers you a position and a salary in favor of one for which you've been told, "We're as good as certain that the funds will be available," know that you're taking a calculated risk.

Timetable for Accepting a Job Offer

Getting Final Information

When you receive an offer is the time to get any additional information that you feel may be necessary to make a good decision. Now that the school is "selling," you can feel free to ask your most probing questions. Be prepared to ask them when you receive an offer, even if you need to schedule another time to talk more extensively. It is not a good idea to call the department again and again asking a different question each time.

Consider visiting the institution a second time to take the opportunity to ask all the questions you can think of about the prospective position and employer. Whether or not you visit, if the prospects for obtaining tenure were not clearly discussed at the campus interview, ask for more detail now. How many tenured and nontenured members does the department have? How many junior faculty members would come up for tenure at the same time you would? How many people have come up for tenure over the last several years? How many were recommended for tenure by the department? How many were granted it? What are the standards the department would expect you to meet in order to recommend it?

If a spouse or partner's job opportunities will be a major factor in your decision, ideally you have already given some indication of that in an earlier interview. Now, however, is the time to find out exactly what the department meant when you were told that "We should be able to find something attractive for him/her." Possibly you will want to arrange for a visit to the area by your partner, if you can persuade the employer to give you that long to reach a decision.

Perhaps you would like to talk to others in the department who were not available on the day that you visited. Perhaps you would like to talk to someone who can knowledgeably discuss local housing and public schools with you. Whatever it is that you feel you need to know, tell the person who makes you the offer so that arrangements can be made for you to obtain the information. Do, however, limit yourself to questions about things that seriously matter to you. If you ask endless questions about what appear to be trivial details, the department may begin to question its judgment in offering you the position.

Negotiating for Time to Consider

Naturally you would like to decide as late as possible, in order to ascertain what other offers you will receive, and the school that offers you a job would like you to accept as early as possible in order to close the search. These competing desires are reconciled through a process of negotiation in which you both agree when you will give the school a binding answer.

Generally this time is measured in weeks. It would be extremely unusual for a school to ask you to decide in less than a week and a two-week limit is more common. Extensions to several weeks are not uncommon, and extensions measured in months are very rare. Before you propose a time to make up your mind, ask the school how long it had planned to give you.

Schools will understand that you may want to see how you have fared in the market. However, if in your interview you have talked enthusiastically about why this school is your first choice, be careful that your behavior now doesn't throw your earlier protestations into doubt. In any case, convey enthusiasm for the offer at the same time as you ask for time to decide. You may take this job and will want to begin it on good terms with your new colleagues.

When Your First Choice Isn't Your First Offer

If you haven't yet had an interview with the school that is your first choice, it's doubtful that you would be able to receive an offer from them before you must accept or reject the job that you have been offered. If you are well into the search process with your first choice, however, it is worthwhile to see whether you can hasten their decision. Furthermore, the information that someone else has offered you a position tends to enhance your credentials.

First negotiate with the school that has offered you the position for as long a decision period as it can give you. If you are willing to take a risk, you may be able to buy the most time by saying, "If you need an immediate answer, I'm afraid it's no." Since this answer may put the offer at risk, it's one you should not give lightly; however, if the school is very serious about getting you, this response does offer the greatest incentive for them to give you a longer time to decide. Then immediately contact your first choice to let them know that you have been offered another position and to ask them what their time frame is. This is most effective if you have already interviewed.

Negotiating

Whether or not you will be able to negotiate successfully for a salary higher than you are initially offered depends upon the institution with which you're negotiating. However, it may be worthwhile to raise the subject. First, be prepared by knowing appropriate salary ranges for this kind of position at this kind of institution. If, in fact, the salary you are offered seems exceptionally high, you may be less inclined to negotiate than if it is low. If you decide to raise the question of salary, the right time to do so is after you are offered the position, but well before the deadline.

Remember that in the period between the time a department offers you a position and the time you accept it, you are a "buyer," in the strongest position to ask for salary or any other special conditions, such as research support, that may be important to you. Make the most of this opportunity by not rushing into agreements you may later regret. You may well be offered a position by phone. If you do not feel comfortable negotiating on the spot, thank the person making the offer, make sure that you understand its basic dimensions, such as salary, and ask if you can get in touch shortly. In the next conversation you can raise any issues that you would like to negotiate and agree on a time by which you will make a decision.

If you decide that you want to try to negotiate a higher salary, what do you do? Begin by expressing enthusiasm for the job and asking whether the department has any flexibility on salary. Usually someone who is prepared to negotiate will answer, even if negatively, in a way that leaves a tiny opening. Note the difference between: "only in highly exceptional and rare cases," and "I'm sorry, but we follow an institution-wide, union-approved, salary pay scale, and there's absolutely nothing we can do about this figure, no matter how interested we are in a candidate."

If you raise the question of salary, be prepared to answer the question, "How much did you have in mind?" Frequently an inquiry on your part will be answered with a response that the person offering you the job will speak with others. This is wonderful, because it gives you both a chance to think further. Take advantage of the opportunity to seek additional advice from faculty members about the figure you have been offered.

Occasionally someone who cannot offer you more salary may be able to offer you other things (or perhaps there are other things that you want more than salary). These could include a reduced teaching load in your first year, special computer or laboratory facilities, funds for travel and summer research, assistance to a spouse who is looking for a job, extra relocation expenses, or something similar. Sometimes no extras at all will be available. Don't hesitate to raise an issue that interests you, but make sure throughout that you maintain a pleasant relationship with the department so that they will remain glad that they offered you the position.

The terms of the offer may change during negotiation. Be sure to have them put in writing so that there is a very clear understanding, and a record of that understanding, between you and the employer as to what has and has not been promised. This isn't simply a method of trying to pin down the chair. Rather it is a way to establish a very clear written record and ensure that you and the department have the same understanding when it comes to teaching load, research support, and so forth. Normally all of these issues will be put in a letter by the chair. However, it's appropriate, if the chair doesn't do that for you, to say, for example, "I look forward to receiving a summary of all these terms in my offer letter." Or, "My offer letter did not include a summary of all the issues that we discussed. Could you please provide that for me?"

Accepting and Rejecting Jobs

At some point you have to decide. Do so with the idea that your decision will be binding for this round of the market. Make your initial acceptance or rejection by phone, then follow up with a letter that confirms what you have said. In a letter of acceptance reaffirm any special conditions that were offered by the department. Once you have accepted, begin to think of yourself as a member of the department and continue to stay in contact with its members until the time you arrive for work.

When you decline a position, do so very politely. Thank the department again for its offer, mention the positive attractions it held for you, and let them know where you will be going. Never burn any bridges. You never know when you will meet the chairman or a faculty member from that department. You never know when the people you turn down may be able to influence the direction of your career. So always stay on good and polite terms with your colleagues in other departments, including departments that you have decided to reject.

If You Do Not Receive an Acceptable Offer on This Round

Some years the job market is better than others. If you are in a very specialized field and come on the market in a year when there are few openings and many outstanding candidates, it may be difficult to obtain a position. At times a candidate will reject the only academic offer he or she receives in a given year, deciding that it would not be wise to take it, whether for personal or for professional reasons. Many fine candidates obtain positions the second time they go on the market. If you know you will face a tight market, begin to formulate a "Plan B" even as you apply for academic positions.

In many cases the best use of your time may be whatever kind of work is most compatible with continuing your research (or finishing your dissertation). The demands of a one-year teaching position are not always conducive to research. On the other hand, if you are interested in a position that stresses teaching and have very little teaching experience, a temporary appointment could be an excellent way to strengthen your credentials.

If you interview for a position for which you think you are particularly well qualified but are not offered the position, consider asking for some constructive feedback. This will work best if you do not seem to be questioning the department's decision. You will need to use your judgment as you listen to any suggestions, realizing that it is unlikely that anyone in the hiring department will share every aspect of the decision with you. Try not to take what you hear personally, but, rather, incorporate any suggestions in your next interview opportunity. Above all, work closely with your advisor as you evaluate offers, make alternative plans, and learn from the interviewing process.

Chapter 17
Additional Considerations

Many of the conventions of academic job hunting developed when most academic disciplines had clear boundaries defined by traditional departmental lines, and most candidates were American men whose spouses, if they had them, did not have careers. As research developments blur traditional disciplinary lines, as candidates in the American academic job market become increasingly diverse in cultural and international backgrounds, and as men and women are increasingly part of two-career couples, job candidates, in many cases, are changing more rapidly than are the departments that will hire them. As has been discussed throughout, as a job candidate, it is best for you to stress the common professional interests and identity that you share with those who may hire you. Examples of this approach follow for three common situations: the job candidate with an interdisciplinary degree, the job candidate who is part of a dual-career couple, and the job candidate who is a foreign national.

Interdisciplinary Areas

If you have an interdisciplinary degree, you have the advantage of being able to apply for jobs in more than one kind of department. On the other hand, when you read job announcements you may notice with dismay that they frequently occur within the confines of departments defined by traditional disciplinary distinctions. At times you may face the problem of seeming "neither fish nor fowl" to a search committee.

If you are looking outside your field, learn the language of that field and use that language in your vita, cover letter, and interview. Disciplines have their own strong identities, and search committees in a related discipline won't consider you if they think you can't talk to them in their language. If at all possible, try to have a letter of recommendation from someone in each discipline in which you are applying.

In addition to those in your own discipline, join other scholarly associations so that you are current academically, as well as aware of job openings. Attend their conferences. To make sure you are aware of all possible openings, ask faculty and recent graduates in the disciplines that interest you for suggestions of places to look for job notices. For example, those in Departments of Folklore may see appropriate jobs listed under English in *The Chronicle of Higher Education* or in the MLA job listings.

Dual-Career Couples

If you are part of a dual-career couple, before you go on the job market you and your partner need to articulate your goals so that you will be able to devise a search strategy that supports your personal and professional goals and to answer potential employers' questions honestly and clearly. Colleges and universities, like other employers, are becoming familiar with candidates coming in pairs. Very often if a department is serious about you, they will do what they can to assist your partner.

Consider the following questions in terms of what's right for the two of you, not what you think an employer wants to hear.

- If one of you has fewer possibilities, perhaps because of being in a very small, specialized field, will that person find a job first, before the other one looks?
- Will you both go on the job market at the same time?
- Will you go only to the same geographic location as your partner?
- What will you do if you both get great job offers but they are on opposite sides of the country?

If you agree that you are willing to apply for and accept positions that are not in the same location, consider the following:

- Can you afford two residences, travel expenses, duplicate household furnishings, and large phone bills?
- Who will do the most commuting? How difficult is travel out of both your and your partner's locations (e.g., a non-stop, two-thousand-mile plane trip may be easier than a three-hundred-mile drive, especially in the snowbelt)?
- If you have children, how will you care for them?
- How good are you at getting along alone? Consider that it will be necessary to be both single and part of a couple at the same time.
- Will your department allow you to concentrate your teaching into two quarters and be away the third? Can you teach only two or three

days per week so as to have long weekends? (Don't ask for these privileges until after you have received an offer.)

It is usually a good idea to reach a joint decision about where both of you will search and within which geographic areas you are each free to act independently. Waiting to discuss these issues until you each have a wonderful job offer in locations thousands of miles apart sets you up for deciding who will "sacrifice" an offer. If the relationship is your priority, it may work out better to decide in advance on geographic locations in which you believe you can both find satisfying employment, whoever gets the first offer, and to concentrate your search on those areas.

If you are considering tenure-track positions, look beyond the first job for your partner to other opportunities. For example, if you are offered a tenure-track position by a university that arranges an attractive postdoctoral position for your partner, consider what you both will want to do after the postdoc has run its course. In general, dual-career couples will find greater opportunities in metropolitan areas, where it may be possible to change jobs without changing locations.

The fact remains that, given the national nature of the academic job market, it is extremely difficult for two academics to make career development their top priority while remaining married to each other. It is particularly difficult if both are in highly specialized areas with very few openings. Accepting at least short periods of geographic separation may help to make it possible, but separation in itself often puts a strain on a relationship. Most people find they need to make a series of choices over the course of a career. The decision you make now will reflect your current priorities and may well be reevaluated as time goes on.

Once you have made your decisions, be very clear with your advisors about how you would prefer that they explain the situation. Be aware that a department wondering whether you will accept a job offer may well make a phone call to someone in your department to ask how your personal situation is likely to affect your acceptance. They may be as likely to call the person they know best in your department as they are to call your advisor, so it is generally to your advantage to have as many people as possible know that you are willing to commute, are committed to a particular geographic location, or whatever else is the case.

Decide at what stage to tell employers that there are two of you: before the interview, during the interview, or after the interview, well before any offer is made. If you will accept or reject an offer totally independently of opportunities for a partner, there is no particular need to discuss your partner's plans at any point of the negotiation.

More commonly, however, your partner's reaction to the location of the position or success in finding a job for himself or herself in that location will be a factor in your decision. In that case, don't wait until you receive an offer to ask about opportunities for a partner.

The way you answer the questions listed above as well as the manner in which you can conduct your job search will vary according to the following factors.

Ph.D. and Ph.D. in the Same Field

Job-sharing may be an option if you are willing to consider it. Hiring institutions, however, may be skeptical about the arrangement unless they have had previous successful experience with it. Before you pursue this option, make every effort to identify some people who have done it successfully, so that you can get some first-hand advice.

More commonly, you each want your own job. If there is any likelihood that you will actually be competing for the same positions, how you will handle the competition is something to consider. If you and your partner are applying to the same department, you may hope that no one will notice that you are attached to each other. Even if you use different names, that is unlikely, given the small-world nature of most academic disciplines. Thus it is also important to let those who are recommending you know how you plan to handle it so that they can help you reinforce that impression. A department that feels it would be "pitting husband and wife against each other" might end up interviewing neither.

Ph.D. and Ph.D. in Different Fields

At some point in the interview you will probably want to tell the search committee that your partner is also looking for a job and see if they will put in a word for him/her with the appropriate department. This practice is becoming increasingly common.

Ph.D. and Non-Ph.D.

When it appears to you that they are seriously considering you for the job, you may wish to tell them about your partner and ask if they can offer any kind of placement assistance, such as names of people to contact. Certainly, if you want help for your partner, ask for assurances about it between the time you are offered a job and the time you accept it.

Non-Traditional Couples

If you are part of an unmarried couple, the same personal considerations will apply. You will also, however, have to consider employers'
probable attitudes toward your relationship. In general, they will probably be willing to do somewhat less for an unmarried partner than for a
married one.

Foreign Nationals Seeking U.S. Employment

First, think realistically about your long-term goals. If you want to work
in the United States only for the duration of your practical training
period, don't apply for tenure-track positions. Instead, concentrate on
short-term appointments, which frequently will carry titles such as
"Visiting Assistant Professor," or "Lecturer." They are less likely than
are tenure-track positions to be nationally advertised, so it may be
worthwhile to make direct inquiries of departments you would like to
join.

Work Permission

If you would like to work in the United States indefinitely, you, and the
department that hires you, will need to deal with the question of work
permission. Generally this is not a great problem in academic hiring,
since academic positions are likely to have very specialized qualifications; this will make it easier for a hiring department to demonstrate to
the U.S. government that it needs you. In addition, most colleges and
universities are familiar enough with the process of hiring foreign
nationals that questions of work permission should not in and of
themselves complicate your search.

However, a great deal of paperwork is involved. Work with the office
on your campus that advises foreign students to see that you handle it
correctly. If your goal is eventual permanent residency or U.S. citizenship, it is particularly important to see that each step of the process is
handled correctly. You may wish to obtain your own legal counsel. If so,
choose the lawyer carefully. Often the campus office that advises foreign students can advise you.

Cultural Differences in the Job Search

You have doubtless become aware of American ways of conducting a
job search during your stay in the United States. However, when you

begin to search for a permanent job you may need to behave in ways that still do not feel entirely appropriate to you. Remember that however supportive your advisor may be, you, rather than your mentor, are expected to make the most effort on your own behalf. You are expected to show initiative during interviews and in meeting new people at conferences or all-day visits to campuses. In interviews, Americans expect that you will speak confidently about yourself and your successes. Making eye contact with even the most senior people will be seen as a sign of confidence rather than of disrespect.

Some of these differences may present challenges to you in preparing for interviews, but console yourself that many Americans do not find the process of job hunting easy either. If you come from a culture in which the assertiveness required in an American job search would appear rude, it is important for you to make a particular effort to talk confidently to others and to initiate conversation. You can do so with confidence that you will almost certainly appear polite.

English

Any institution, whether it emphasizes teaching or research, will probably pay considerable attention to your ability to speak, communicate, and write. Writing and speaking are just as important to research as they are to teaching. If your ability to write and speak English is weak, tutoring will be helpful. To prepare for a specific interview, try what one enterprising job candidate did. Knowing that he did not have time before a critical interview to change his whole way of speaking, he made a list of the words he used most frequently in describing his work, had a native speaker tape them for him, and then practiced enunciating them again and again.

If your written English is correct but not colloquial, have a native-speaker read drafts of your cover letters. Hiring departments will assume that your written English is at least as good as, if not better than, your spoken English, so be sure cover letters are both correct and colloquial. Pay particular attention to the section on cover letter writing in this guide. American-style cover letters may be less formal than those you would write at home.

Part V
After You Take the Job

Chapter 18
Starting the Job

You have received and accepted an offer. You are excited about the successful job search, about your new employer, and about planning for the upcoming year. It's time to prepare for the new job so you can get off to a good start as a tenure-track professor. A successful beginning will probably result in a successful first year and will help you in the long road toward tenure.

Moving to Your New Job

In most cases, the new professor leaves the city where he or she did graduate work. Plan to move to your new institution one and a half to two months before school starts. That means you should start looking for a place to live in April or May. After you accept the job, contact the college or university housing office for information on faculty housing. If you are moving a family and need to consider a spouse's job or school or daycare for children, have the housing office recommend a realtor or relocation company that can help meet these needs. Get the names of a couple of recently hired people in your department and ask them for housing suggestions. Also ask for help with your spouse's job hunt. Most institutions can provide some assistance here. Try to get moved in and settled in July.

Get to know your way around the campus and the town or city. Become familiar with public transportation and driving so you can determine the most efficient way for you to get to classes.

If you haven't already done so, complete your dissertation. It's very important to have that behind you so you can devote your energy to your new teaching and research responsibilities. Set deadlines for yourself and finish it before classes begin.

Getting Ready to Teach

While it's summer and things are more relaxed, get to know the staff and learn how the department works. Learn now: how to get things photocopied; when to place materials on reserve; when departmental meetings are held and whether junior faculty attend them. See what your teaching schedule is and start to think about setting up office hours. What are office procedures and deadlines? How are books ordered from the bookstore? Visit and become familiar with the library. Before classes start and life becomes hectic, get a sense of the timetables.

Try to get to know your new colleagues. Usually there are lots of junior faculty around because they do not have money to go away. Set up some lunch or coffee dates and get advice. Ask them what they wished they'd known when they started. Learn as much as you can about both formal structures such as classes, and informal structures such as how information is passed on through the department. Discuss students' abilities and expected workloads so you can plan your classes accordingly. If it's likely that you will be teaching large classes, find out how many students must be in a course before it is assigned a teaching assistant.

Every department and school has its own history and its own way of doing things. Listen carefully to everything you are told, but be careful to form your own opinions. If you feel you are hearing only one side of a story, take care to learn the other. While you are still new, try to establish a comfortable basis for communication with everyone in the department. Some of the people who will influence your ability to be productive are not fellow faculty, but the staff people in your department and school. They include secretaries, librarians, business staff, janitors, computing center staff, and the people who staff laboratory facilities. These people can help you greatly or make your life miserable. You should value their contributions and get to know them.

Your Own Research

You will probably have very little time first semester to do your own work. Your time will fill up with departmental responsibilities as well as teaching. However, you can base some of your courses on your own research and, possibly, teach your dissertation for your first graduate level course.

You will be asked about your research, so try to keep thinking about it even if you can't really work on it. Try to have one day or a half day a week away from the office for your own work. If you are used to working closely with your advisor, you may miss the stimulus of that interaction, as well as the structure imposed when you work with someone else. Of course, you will want to keep in touch with your advisor, but start thinking about others with whom you wish to collaborate or with whom you wish to discuss your ideas. You can use deadlines for calls for papers as a way of giving yourself a realistic schedule for your work. If no one but you knows or cares about your research and you face no deadlines, you risk putting day-to-day demands ahead of the more major goals you wish to accomplish.

Teaching

With teaching you will have to make policies for your students and stick to them. Before questions arise, think about how you are going to keep order. Are you going to grant extensions and under what circumstances? How will you grade work? What are guidelines for grading in the department? Talk with other faculty and get suggestions.

Be as organized a teacher as possible. Do your lecture notes in whatever style best suits you. Keep your notes from year to year. If possible, write them on a computer so you can both easily change them and keep them. Avoid teaching new courses in the spring. Instead, offer new subjects in the fall when you will have had the summer to prepare.

You may be given a big class that no one else wants, such as a survey or introductory course. Try to put your personal stamp on it and make it your own, yet, at the same time, don't feel you have to know everything. If you haven't had much experience preparing lectures, talk with some of your new colleagues or some of your former professors from your graduate institution. One suggestion is to take one or two ideas and pursue them in a lot of detail. Write a short lecture and prepare a few good questions to ask the students. Find out if your institution offers any teaching help to new professors such as videotaping.

Students

In addition to developing your teaching style, think about your students. In many institutions they are 17 to 22 years old and come with problems that go with that age. They are involved in themselves: trying to figure out who they are, academically, socially, politically, and personally. Academic matters are not their only concern. You may also have older students in your class whose lives and goals are quite different from those of the younger, traditional students. Develop an approach that will reach these students.

Be Critical

At the end of the first year evaluate your teaching and consider your own observations as well as those of other faculty and students. Decide what you want to do differently and incorporate those changes as you begin planning for the second year. Get an informal discussion group going with other junior faculty and share ideas on successful teaching.

Departmental Responsibilities

It is important that you get involved in the life of your department and take on some responsibilities that feel important such as directing honors students, freshman advising, or running the colloquium series. Choose carefully a few responsibilities and do them really well. Then you can say no to other things including university service. Try not to get involved in university committees during your first few years so you can concentrate on teaching and research.

A Mentor

Try to develop a relationship with a senior professor who can help you out as you feel your way through the first year. Ask him or her to visit one of your classes and then give you feedback. Also find out how your colleagues perceive you. Are you seen as fitting into the department? Are you seen as carrying your load? Are you seen as productive? As an assistant professor you are entitled to regular discussions with the chair and senior people as to how you are doing. Such regular feedback will help you keep on track in the process of obtaining tenure.

Chapter 19
Knowing About and Getting Tenure

Most institutions have some form of tenure. When you interviewed for your job or during the acceptance discussion, you probably asked some questions about tenure at your new institution. Before you begin working, it's helpful to know how many junior faculty are granted tenure, both within your department and university-wide. If 80 percent of the faculty in the whole school are tenured, the possibility for tenure for new Ph.D.'s is limited.

The movement for the tenure system began in the early 1900s and became very strong after World War I. It was developed to provide faculty with freedom of expression. Proponents of tenure believe it is healthy for the nation to have a body of individuals who can say what they want and be protected. Opponents of tenure believe it protects the incompetent, among other things.

The tenure system allows the new assistant professor a chance to grow comfortable with the institution, with teaching, and with research. It allows the institution an opportunity to evaluate his or her work. The usual span of time before making the tenure decision is six years, with tenure granted or denied in the seventh. Some places, however, go eight or nine years before making the decision.

Criteria used to determine tenure also vary from place to place. At a major research institution, research publications are most important. Quality, not quantity, is the issue. Usually at least one book and some articles in juried publications are necessary in the humanities and social sciences, while several journal articles are crucial in the sciences. The department may count only certain journals, so be sure to know which are considered important. Often, particularly in the sciences and engineering, much of your success will be determined by your effectiveness in raising funds to support your research. Concentrate on research, publication, and teaching—in that order.

At a small liberal arts college, teaching is the most significant criterion. At such a school you should refine your teaching skills and develop your own personal teaching style that is both well received by students and ensures that they learn.

Example of the Tenure Process at a Large Research Institution

The tenure process is different in each institution and it is important that you learn early what the process is for you. The following illustrates the process at one large research institution.

Appointments

Appointments for assistant professors are made for three or four years, to be renewed for three years. Review for promotion comes up after six years and is quite lengthy and complicated.

The Review Process

At the beginning of the sixth year, the review process begins in the department with the appointment of a three to four person subcommittee (all tenured faculty). The committee collects publications and teaching records from the candidate as well as oral and written recommendations from inside and outside the university. After these items are reviewed, the department has a meeting to take a formal vote.

Letters of support from outside the institution are very important. The department puts together a list of outside reviewers who are prominent people in the field. This list is reviewed at the dean's level and later at the provost's.

If the departmental vote is favorable, the chair writes a letter that includes the majority and minority opinions, adds his or her own opinion, and sends the letter with the review materials to the dean.

The dean refers the packet of material to a personnel committee composed of tenured faculty. This committee has three subcommittees: humanities, social sciences, and natural sciences. The subcommittee reads everything and makes recommendations to the committee as a whole. If this committee includes a member of the candidate's department, he or she will not participate in the discussion and will not vote but will answer questions. The chief job of this committee is to look at outside letters to see if the research is judged important. When the committee has voted, the dean writes a letter and sends the results on to the provost.

The provost gives the materials to a committee consisting of deans and other senior administrators. This group reads the outside letters and examines the financial base for the position since most tenure decisions involve more than a million dollars over a period of time. After a vote is taken, the materials go to the president.

The president reviews the files and usually accepts the provost's decision. The president takes the decision to the trustees who act formally and legally on the case. A letter from the trustees comes to the successful candidate a few months after the decision.

The process can take months because it takes a long time to get the outside letters.

Example of the Tenure Process at a Small Teaching College

At one small, private college where the emphasis is on excellent teaching, the tenure process is somewhat different.

There are three evaluations before tenure. The first is after two years and weeds out any hiring mistakes. The second is held in the fourth year and is becoming increasingly important. The third is for making the tenure decision and is held at the beginning of the sixth year.

For all evaluations—including, later on, for full professor—there are three criteria: teaching, professional development, and collegiate citizenship. Teaching is the most important. Professional development, which includes publications, has become increasingly important whereas it used to be equal in importance to collegiate citizenship. Collegiate citizenship is mainly committee work but also includes recruiting students, alumni activities, and advising some student organizations.

All faculty are invited to visit the candidate's classes and write letters of recommendation. However, recommendations from the candidate's departmental colleagues matter the most, with those of tenured faculty carrying the most weight. The candidate and department chair come up with a list of other persons from whom letters are requested. These include scholars at other institutions, students, and recent alumni. A dossier of letters is sent to the provost who makes a recommendation to the president by a certain date. The formal power for granting tenure then lies with the Board of Trustees who meet near the end of the academic year. The candidate learns the result immediately.

Advice

The years until tenure consideration will be the toughest in your academic life. Concentrate on research and teaching. Try to avoid being department chair or serving on many committees until you have tenure, unless you know for sure that your institution weighs such service heavily in tenure decisions. If you are the only woman or minority person in your department, your presence on all kinds of committees will be sought. Learn to say no to most requests. Know the tenure criteria well before you have to provide documentation that you have fulfilled them. At many institutions, teaching records are important. Letters are requested from students and recent alumni. Save teaching recommendations and start building that file early.

Seek a mentor within the department who can keep you apprised of your progress. Listen seriously to that person's feedback. Make an effort to talk with others in the department to let them know what you are doing. Talk with others about your teaching and about good classes so that your colleagues perceive you as a strong teacher. Remain in touch with others in the field at other institutions in case you need external referees. Send them drafts of papers, solicit their advice, meet them at conferences.

Usually the candidate knows at what stage of the review process he or she is. If it begins to look increasingly unlikely that you will be awarded tenure, you may want to start looking at other jobs before the formal evaluation process begins.

Try to keep the whole process in perspective. Tenure decisions ultimately involve many variables, some of which, such as an institution's financial situation, have nothing to do with a candidate's abilities. Hiring committees at other institutions are fully aware of that. So if you do not obtain tenure, you will do what many other highly competent people in that situation have done. You will obtain another position and continue with a productive career.

Meanwhile, the whole tenure process typically occurs when you are building in other areas of your life as well. You may be raising a family, buying your first house, meeting obligations to other family members, building a strong network of friendships that are deeply meaningful to you. You will not have unlimited time for these other areas of life, but don't neglect them either. Not only are they important in and of themselves, but the perspective that comes from realizing there's more to life than the next paper frequently makes the time you spend working more creative and productive.

Chapter 20
Changing Jobs

At some point you may decide or need to change jobs. There can be many reasons for changing jobs, and each will require slightly different job-seeking strategies.

Perhaps you originally wanted to work at a different type of institution but were unable to find such a position during your original job hunt. Or, for one reason or another, you planned to stay for only a few years. Maybe you feel that the institution hasn't lived up to its original commitment to you in terms of lab space, research assistance, library funding, or something else that was negotiated during the offer. Possibly you have been approached by another institution. Possibly your spouse or another family member is unhappy with the location or institution and the situation cannot be improved for him/her. If you have been conducting a long-distance marriage or relationship for several years, you may have decided that being together is more important than your job.

Be Ready for Opportunities

Continue to stay in touch with people at other institutions, even if you are very happy where you are. These contacts are a vital means of engaging in your profession. In addition, knowing faculty at other institutions gives you greater access to information about positions that may be opening up, and a group of people who can comment favorably on your work.

If you come from an institution that has a credentials file service, continue to build a file of letters even if you don't ever expect to move. It's a form of insurance that you can draw on if you decide you must or want to change positions.

Keep your vita current. Until you are very senior you will probably continue to keep your education as the first item. However, if previously you gave a lot of detail about your graduate work, you may now begin to omit it. For at least several years after obtaining your doctorate, however, retain your dissertation topic and advisor's name. Add recent experiences and condense earlier ones. For example, if you earlier included detail about what you did as a teaching assistant, you may now merely retain the notation that you held the position. In general, it is a good idea to condense items, even if drastically, rather than to drop them altogether. Do not drop early publications and presentations.

If You Want to Make a Move

Keep in mind that academia is a small world and if you put out feelers, chances are your department will hear about it. Mention in cover letters that you don't want your institution contacted unless you are considered a very serious contender. You will need someone to recommend you. While it is true that you can send out letters in a credentials file without the knowledge of the letters' authors, there is no guarantee that at least one of these people will not get a phone call about you. Therefore, it is a better idea to speak with your recommenders, let them know what you are interested in, and ask them to keep your search confidential. Your advisor, of course, is an ideal person to play this role. It would be helpful to have a recommendation from someone in your current department. You will have to use your best judgment about the advisability of letting someone there know your plans.

If you begin interviewing extensively, it is almost inevitable that your department will learn that you are looking elsewhere. It will depend very much upon the individuals involved whether they view this as perfectly reasonable activity or a lack of commitment. In any case, it is preferable that the chair hear from you, rather than from someone else, that you are looking. You may want to defer this communication until you are almost certain that the person is about to have the information anyway. Never use the threat that you will look elsewhere as a negotiating point. If you do not find another position quickly after making such a threat, your bluff will have been called forever.

To make such a move responsibly, minimize new commitments, such as agreeing to supervise a doctoral thesis, in which your departure at year's end would seriously compromise someone else's plans.

If You Have to Move

A very common reason for changing jobs in academia is that of not getting tenure or of being very certain that it will not be awarded. Or it may be that you have accepted a short-term, non-renewable position. In either case you will not need to keep your search quiet within the department, and you may find some very active allies there as you conduct your search.

If you felt it was likely that you would be awarded tenure and you were not, it is almost inevitable that you will feel intensely disappointed. You may also feel very angry or depressed or experience a sense of personal failure. These feelings are natural and will run their course. Try to make every effort, however, to minimize their effect on your professional behavior. If you can deal with department members and interview as if you are confident and happy about your future prospects, you will receive more positive feedback and results which, in turn, will make you genuinely feel better. Meanwhile, outside of work, take up karate, spend time with friends and family, seek help from a counselor, become involved in community service, or do whatever else your experience has shown you is restorative for you.

Don't lose any time in applying for jobs as soon as you find you will need to look. While you may have some impulse to avoid other department members after receiving a negative tenure decision, now is precisely the time you should be talking to them. Ask your strongest supporters if they will be willing to recommend you. Let everyone know the kinds of jobs you will be looking for, and ask people to let you know of openings they hear about. Give strongly interested and supportive people copies of your vita.

Let all your professional contacts know that you are in the market. It is most comfortable for all concerned if you take the responsibility for obtaining information. For example, rather than asking people to "keep you in mind," ask whether they can suggest whom you might call at a specific institution, what they have heard lately about a particular department, if they know someone that they might be willing to call on your behalf at an institution where you have applied, and so forth. Keep in touch about your search with those who seem enthusiastically supportive of it. If you sense that others are lukewarm, continue to keep in touch on a professional basis, but don't pursue the topic of your search with them.

When Someone Else Wants You to Move

A different kind of reason for changing jobs is that of an unsolicited advance by another institution. It's attractive to be sought out, so, if you decide to move, keep your wits and negotiate a good offer from the institution that is pursuing you. If you don't want to move, this is a great opportunity to give your institution a chance to keep you, through increased salary, an early, favorable tenure decision, or whatever else you might choose to negotiate for.

Be aware, however, that, unless your work is truly world-class, this is an exercise you will not be able to repeat very frequently. Whenever you say, "I will take this offer unless you do X," there is a possibility that your employer will say, "We'll be sorry to lose you, but it looks as if you had best take the offer, because we certainly can't do that." As when you negotiated for your first salary, begin with open-ended questions, and don't give ultimatums unless you are willing to stand behind them.

The Graceful Exit

As soon as you have accepted an offer at another institution, let your department know. Do everything you can to tie up loose ends in terms of responsibilities to other people. If there are those in the department to whom you are genuinely grateful, be sure to express your appreciation. If you can't wait to leave every person there behind you, at a minimum, be courteous. Satisfying as you might fantasize it would be to tell everyone exactly what you think before you leave, doing so would almost certainly be something you would later regret.

After you leave, keep in touch with people with whom you have enjoyed working. The opportunity to build a rich network of contacts, to have a group of people who live all over the country, and possibly the world, whom you know you will always enjoy seeing at an annual meeting, with whom you can correspond and exchange ideas, is one of the rewards of the academic career you have chosen.

Appendices

Appendix 1: National Job Listings Sources and Scholarly and Professional Associations

Periodicals That Include Job Listings of Interest to All Scholars

Black Issues in Higher Education
published every two weeks (26 issues per year)

Cox Matthews & Associates, Inc.
10520 Warwick Ave.
Suite B-8
Fairfax, VA 22030

(703) 385–2981

This magazine covers a wide range of issues in higher education and how they affect blacks and other minorities. An annual special report covers careers in higher education, including salaries. Many pages of each issue are devoted to faculty and administration position announcements from institutions across the United States and abroad.

The Chronicle of Higher Education
published weekly (48 issues per year)

1255 23rd St., N.W.
Washington, DC 20037

(202) 466–1000

This is the newspaper of higher education. Articles cover all aspects of teaching, research, administration, and student life. Focus is on American higher education with additional coverage on the rest of the world. Grant deadlines, faculty promotions, and book reviews are included.

The "Bulletin Board" has extensive listings for faculty and administrative position announcements, from institutions all over the world, primarily from the United States. Announcements are listed in two ways: (1) an alphabetical listing by subject and (2) display ads with an accompanying index.

Selected Scholarly and Professional Associations

For each association listed here you will find association name, address, phone number, discipline(s) it serves, title and frequency of job listings, time of the annual convention, description of convention placement services, and title of discipline-specific handout on job-hunting if there is one. Many associations include job listings in the association newsletter. Some associations have a separate job listing available to members and non-members for an additional charge. It is often possible to have job listings sent first class for an additional fee. If the organizations relevant to your discipline are not listed here, consult *National Trade and Professional Associations* and your advisor.

Academy of Management
P.O. Box 39
Ada, OH 45810

(419) 772–1953

Management

Placement Roster, twice a year to members only.

Convention held in August. Interviewing space is made available.

American Academy of Religion
501 Hall of Languages
Syracuse University
Syracuse, NY 13244–1170

(315) 443–4019

Religious Studies, Theology, Ministry

Openings: *Job Opportunities for Scholars of Religion*, 6 times a year for an additional charge.

Convention usually held in November. Placement Assistance Center provides interviewing space. Interviews set up by employers and candidates.

American Anthropological Association
1703 New Hampshire Ave., N.W.
Washington, DC 20009

(202) 232–8800

Anthropology

Anthropology Newsletter, 9 times a year to members.

Placement Service Notes, 8–10 issues per year, extra charge for members and non-members. Includes job listings as well as short articles on job hunting strategies.

Convention usually held in November. Job listings are posted and persons can apply at the convention. Space is provided for interviewing.

American Astronomical Society
2000 Florida Ave., N.W.
Suite 300
Washington, DC 20009

(202) 328–2010

Astronomy, Astrophysics

American Astronomical Society Job Register, monthly to members.

Conventions usually held in January and June. A Job Center is set up to get applicants and employers together.

American Chemical Society
1155 16th St., N.W.
Washington, DC 20036

(202) 872–4600

Chemistry, Chemical Engineering

Chem Jobs USA, weekly to members and non-members for an additional charge.

Convention time varies. Career placement register provides access to jobs by computer. Candidates register with the ACS and send vitas.

American Economic Association
2014 Broadway, Suite 305
Nashville, TN 37203

(615) 322–2595

Economics

Job Openings for Economists, every other month to members and non-members for a separate subscription.

Convention usually held in December or January. There is a placement service run by the National Registry for Economists, (312) 793–4904.

American Educational Research Association
1230 17th St., N.W.
Washington, DC 20036

(202) 223–9485

Education

Convention held in the spring. Interview facilities are made avilable.

American Folklore Society
c/o American Anthropological Association
1703 New Hampshire Avenue, N.W.
Washington, DC 20009

(202) 232–8800

Folklore

AFS Newsletter, monthly to members.

Convention usually held in October.

American Historical Association
400 A St., S.E.
Washington, DC 20003

(202) 544–2422

History, Ancient History, American Studies, and other area studies, and history professionals such as archivists and librarians.

Perspectives, monthly during the academic year, to members.

Convention held in December. Job Register for pre-arranged interviews usually advertised in *Perspectives*.

Careers for Students in History.

American Institute of Biological Sciences
730 11th St., N.W.
Washington, DC 20001–4521

(202) 628–1500

Biology (does not include Medical Biology or Biotechnology)

Job listings in *Bioscience*, a monthly.

Convention held in August. Résumé Board where candidates can post résumés and employers can post job listings. The organization does not set up interviews.

Careers in Biology.

American Institute of Chemical Engineers
345 E. 47th St.
New York, NY 10017

(212) 705-7338

Chemical Engineering

Has computerized Job Referral Service.

Convention held three times a year.

American Mathematical Society
Box 6248
Providence, RI 02940

(401) 272-9500

Mathematics

Notices of the American Mathematical Society, monthly to all members.

Employment Information in the Mathematical Sciences, 7 times a year, extra charge for members and non-members.

Convention held in January. Employment Register organizes formal interviewing.

Seeking Employment in the Mathematical Sciences.

American Musicological Society
201 S. 34th St.
Philadelphia, PA 19104

(215) 898-8698

Music

Convention in October or November.

American Philological Association
Department of Classics
Holy Cross College
Worcester, MA 01610

(508) 793–2547

Classical Studies, Classical Languages, Ancient History, Linguistics

Positions for Classicists and Archaeologists, monthly for a separate charge.

Convention is usually held in late December. Interviews are scheduled by the association.

Careers for Classicists.

American Philosophical Association
University of Delaware
Newark, DE 19716

(302) 451–1112

Philosophy

Jobs for Philosophers, 5 times a year to members only.

Three conventions a year: eastern U.S. in December (largest), west coast in March, central U.S. in April. A placement service is held at each one. Through a mailbox system, candidates leave vitas and request interviews and universities notify them.

American Physical Society
335 East 45th St.
New York, NY 10017

(212) 682–7341

Physics

Summary of Open Positions, 9 times a year for an additional charge.

Conventions held in March and April. Set up by affiliate association, American Institute of Physics, (212) 661–9404 (same address). Applicants can leave vitas for employers and interview space is made available.

American Planning Association
1776 Massachusetts Ave., N.W.
Washington, DC 20036

(202) 872–0611

City and Regional Planning

Job Mart Magazine, twice a month for a separate subscription.

Annual convention in March or April.

American Political Science Association
1527 New Hampshire Ave., N.W.
Washington, DC 20036

(202) 483–2512

Political Science, International Relations, American Government, Public Administration

APSA Personnel Service Newsletter, monthly to members only.

Convention held in August. Candidates may leave vitas on file and interviewing space is made available.

American Psychological Association
1200 17th St., N.W.
Washington, DC 20036

(202) 955–7600

Psychology

APA Monitor, monthly to members.

Convention held in August. Applicants can file vitas and employers can advertise positions. Message system. Employers set up own interviews but interview space is provided.

American Society of Civil Engineers
345 E. 47th St.
New York, NY 10017

(212) 705–7496

Civil Engineering

Convention held in October.

American Sociological Association
1722 N St., N.W.
Washington, DC 20036

(202) 833–3410

Sociology

Employment Bulletin, monthly for an additional charge.

Convention held in August. Employers submit job descriptions and set up interviews.

American Statistical Association
1429 Duke St.
Alexandria, VA 22314–3402

(703) 684–1221

Statistics

AMSTAT News, monthly to members. Available to non-members for a charge.

Convention held in August. Employers and applicants pre-register for placement service. Interview space is made available.

American Studies Association
2140 Taliaferro Hall
University of Maryland
College Park, MD 20742

(301) 405–1364

American Civilization, English, History

ASA Newsletter, quarterly to members.

Convention held first week of November. Serves as a job clearinghouse. Makes vitas available to prospective employers. Makes space available for interviews but does not set up appointments.

Archaeological Institute of America
675 Commonwealth Ave.
Boston, MA 02215

(617) 353–9361

Archaeology

Convention usually held in December.

Associated Writing Programs
Old Dominion University
Norfolk, VA 23508

(804) 683–3839

English, Writing

AWP Job List, monthly to members.

Association for Asian Studies
1 Lane Hall
University of Michigan
Ann Arbor, MI 48109

(313) 665–2490

China and Inner Asia Studies, Northeast Asia Studies, South Asia Studies, and Southeast Asia Studies

"Personnel Registry" in *AAS Newsletter*, 5 issues a year to members.

Convention is in the spring. Candidates and employers can register and set up interviews.

Association of Collegiate Schools of Architecture
1735 New York Ave., N.W.
Washington, DC 20006

(202) 785–2324

Architecture

ACSA News, monthly during the academic year.

Convention usually held in March or April.

Association of Schools of Journalism and Mass Communication
1621 College St.
Columbia, SC 29208–0251

(803) 777–2005

Journalism, Broadcast Communications, Public Relations, Advertising

AEJMC News, 6 times a year for a separate charge.

Convention is held in August. Job listings, résumé books, and interviewing space are made available.

College Art Association of America
275 Seventh Ave.
New York, NY 10001

(212) 691–1051

Fine Arts (Studio), History of Art

Position Listings, 6 times a year to members. Available to non-members for a charge.

Convention time varies. Interviewing space is made available.

Council on Social Work Education
1600 Duke St.
Alexandria, VA 22314

(703) 683–8080

Social Work

Teachers Registry and Information Service, 3 times a year to members. Available to non-members for a charge.

Convention held in March. Job listings and vitas are made available.

Federation of American Societies for Experimental Biology
9650 Rockville Pike
Bethesda, MD 20814

(301) 530–7000

Biomedical Sciences

Federation of scientific societies:
American Association of Immunologists—(301) 530–7178
American Association of Pathologists—(301) 530–7130
American Institute of Nutrition—(301) 530–7050
American Physiological Society—(301) 530–7164
American Society for Biochemistry and Molecular Biology—(301) 530–7145
American Society for Cell Biology—(301) 530–7153
American Society for Pharmacology and Experimental Therapeutics—(301) 530–7060

"Employment Opportunities" in each issue of the *FASEB Journal*, monthly for an additional charge.

Convention held in April. Provide interview scheduling, notification, and space, and vita/application referral.

Geological Society of America
3300 Penrose Place, Box 9140
Boulder, CO 80301

(303) 447–2020

Geology

Convention held in October. Vitas can be input into a computer database. Space for interviewing is provided.

Gerontological Society of America
1275 K St., N.W., Suite 350
Washington, DC 20005–4006

(202) 842–1275

Social Gerontology, Sociology

Newsletter, monthly to members. Available to non-members for a charge.

Convention held in November. Employers and applicants register in advance. Vitas are compiled and made available by category. Interviewing space is provided.

History of Science Society
NMAH, Rm. 5000
Smithsonian Institute
Washington, DC 20560

(202) 357–2274

History and Sociology of Science and Medicine

Newsletter, quarterly to membership.

Convention in the fall or December. Interviewing space is made available.

Institute of Electrical and Electronics Engineers
345 E. 47th St.
New York, NY 10017

(221) 705–7867

Electrical/Electronics Engineering

International Communication Association
Box 9589
Austin, TX 78766

(512) 454–8299

Communications

ICA Newsletter, quarterly to membership.

Convention held in May.

Linguistics Society of America
1325 18th St., N.W.
Suite 211
Washington, DC 20036

(202) 835–1714

Linguistics

"Job Opportunities" is part of the *LSA Bulletin*, 4 times a year to members.

Convention is in January. Announcements and vitas are collected and space is made available for interviewing.

Materials Research Society
9800 McKnight Rd., Suite 327
Pittsburgh, PA 15237

(412) 367–3003

Materials Science

MRS Bulletin, monthly to members.

Two conventions: west coast in spring, east coast after Thanksgiving.

Modern Language Association of America
10 Astor Place
New York, NY 10003

(212) 475–9500

English, Comparative Literature, Modern Languages and Literatures

Job Information List, 4 times a year for a separate charge.

Convention is held in December. At the sign-in center department chairpersons leave their conference locations; pre-arranged interviews are held in a large room; message-center for late notices.

Population Association of America
1722 N. St., N.W.
Washington, DC 20036

(202) 429–0891

Demography

PAA Affairs, quarterly to members. Non-members may subscribe.

Convention held in March. Employment Exchange. Interviewing space made available.

Regional Science Association
Rm. 1–3 Observatory
University of Illinois
901 S. Mathews
Urbana, IL 61801

(217) 333–8904

Regional Science

Newsletter, 3 times a year to members.

Society for Industrial and Applied Mathematics
3600 University City Science Center
Philadelphia, PA 19104–2688

(215) 382–9800

Mathematics

SIAM News. Bimonthly to members. Non-members may subscribe.

Conference held in July.

Scholarly associations exist for other disciplines not listed here.

Discipline Index to Major Scholarly Associations

American Civilization/American Studies: American Historical Association, American Studies Association

Ancient History: American Historical Association, American Philological Association

Anthropology: American Anthropological Association

Archaeology: Archaeological Institute of America

Architecture: Association of Collegiate Schools of Architecture

Area Studies: American Historical Association, Association for Asian Studies

Astronomy: American Astronomical Society

Astrophysics: American Astronomical Society

Biology: American Institute of Biological Sciences, Federation of American Societies for Experimental Biology

Biomedical Sciences: Federation of American Societies for Experimental Biology

Chemistry: American Chemical Society

City Planning: American Planning Association

Classical Archaeology: Archaeological Institute of America

Classical Languages/Classical Studies: American Philological Association

Communications: Association of Schools of Journalism and Mass Communication, International Communication Association

Comparative Literature: Modern Language Association of America

Demography: Population Association of America

Economics: American Economic Association

Education: American Educational Research Association

Engineering: American Chemical Society, American Physical Society, Institute of Electrical and Electronics Engineers, American Society of Civil Engineers, American Institute of Chemical Engineers, Materials Research Society

English: American Studies Association, Associated Writing Programs, Modern Language Association of America

Fine Arts: College Art Association of America

Folklore: American Folklore Society

Geology: Geological Society of America

Gerontology: Gerontological Society of America

Government: American Political Science Association

Greek: American Philological Association

History: American Historical Association, American Studies Association

History of Art: College Art Association of America

History of Science: History of Science Society

International Relations: American Political Science Association

Journalism: Association of Schools of Journalism and Mass Communication

Languages/Literature, Modern: Modern Language Association of America

Latin: American Philological Association

Linguistics: American Philological Association, Linguistics Society of America, Modern Language Association of America

Management: Academy of Management

Mathematics: American Mathematical Society, Society for Industrial and Applied Mathematics

Music: American Musicological Society

Philosophy: American Philosophical Association

Physics: American Physical Society

Political Science: American Political Science Association

Psychology: American Psychological Association

Regional Planning: American Planning Association

Regional Science: Regional Science Association

Religious Studies: American Academy of Religion

Social Work: Council on Social Work Education

Sociology: American Sociological Association

Statistics: American Statistical Association

Theology: American Academy of Religion

Appendix 2: Additional Reading

This selective listing is provided to give you ideas about the type of additional reading that may help you in your job search. It is not intended to be a comprehensive bibliography. For current articles on topics such as the job market in your field, trends in higher education, and academic life, consult your professional association and the ERIC database. An enormous amount has also been written about career theory and about higher education. For reading in these more general areas, consult your library.

General

Anthony, Rebecca and Gerald Roe. *Finding a Job in Your Field: A Handbook for Ph.D.'s and M.A.'s*. Princeton, N.J.: Peterson's Guides, 1984.
 A book for Ph.D.'s seeking either academic or non-academic positions. The vita and letters chapters include many examples of written materials from various kinds of candidates. A chapter on obstacles and options includes re-entering the job market, job-sharing, and looking for a job when you have been fired.

Deneef, A. Leigh, Craufurd D. Goodwin, and Ellen Stern McCrate, eds. *The Academic's Handbook*. Durham, N.C.: Duke University Press, 1988.
 Twenty-two chapters written by several professors to describe the structure of the academic career and the life of an academic. Section Two, "Academic Employment," covers getting a job, an overview of the job market, the tenure system and getting tenure, and academic salaries and benefits. Other sections are on teaching, getting funding, and publishing.

Gaus, Paula J. and others. "The Academic Interview." *Journal of College Placement*, vol. 43, no. 2 (Winter 1983), 61–62, 64–65.
 A list of questions that candidates for academic jobs should be prepared to ask and answer.

Rose, Suzanne, ed. *The Career Guide for Women Scholars*. New York: Springer, 1986.

A guide for women considering academic careers. Issues covered include negotiating in what has been a male-dominated world, recognizing and dealing with discrimination, and attaining tenure.

Rosovsky, Henry. *The University: An Owner's Manual*. New York: W.W. Norton, 1990.
A lively, knowledgeable, and eminently readable account of how a major university works. The author has served as Dean of the Faculty of Arts and Sciences at Harvard University.

Verba, Cynthia. *Scholarly Pursuits: A Practical Guide to Academe*. Cambridge, Mass.: Harvard University, Graduate School of Arts and Sciences, Office of Student Affairs and Office of Career Services, 1987.
An overview of the academic profession written for students at Harvard. This book descibes doctoral programs, how to apply for teaching positions, and how to apply for fellowships. Samples, with commentary, of vitas, cover letters, thesis abstracts and job listings are included for teaching and research positions.

Humanities/Arts

Rice, Roberta W. *Finding a Job in Higher Education in Art Education*. Reston, Va.: National Art Education Association, 1986.
A discussion of job search strategies for fine artists seeking academic jobs. Includes preparation of vita, cover letter, slides and portfolio.

Showalter, English, revised by. *A Career Guide for PhDs and PhD Candidates in English and Foreign Languages*. New York: Modern Language Association, 1985.
A guide for language and literature Ph.D.'s. The chapter, "The Academic Job Search" is extensive. It covers sources of job information, how to apply, written materials, letters of recommendation as well as interviewing—before, during and after, and job negotiations. One section addresses experienced candidates. There are also chapters on community and junior colleges and advice to departments.

Science/Engineering

Jones, Marilyn S., John G. Casali, and Timothy J. Greene. "The New Educator: Criteria for Selecting a University Engineering Faculty Position." *Engineering Education*, vol. 75, no. 7 (April 1985), 624, 626, 628.
A very comprehensive list of questions candidates might ask when selecting a faculty position. Many questions might easily be generalized to other fields.

Lewis, Adele. *The Best Résumés for Scientists and Engineers*. New York: John Wiley and Sons, 1988.
A general discussion. While this book does not specifically address academic employment, many of the sample résumés it provides could be easily adapted to vita format.

Traweek, Sharon. *Beamtimes and Lifetimes: The World of High Energy Physicists.* Cambridge, Mass.: Harvard University Press, 1988.

An ethnographer's view of scientific research. All readers may be interested in the chapters that discuss the stages a scientist passes through on the way from undergraduate physics major to independent researcher. Women in traditionally male disciplines will find the entire discussion interesting, as will anyone interested in the sociology of knowledge.

Social Sciences

Zanna, Mark P. and John M. Darley, eds. *The Compleat Academic: A Practical Guide for the Beginning Social Scientist.* New York: Random House, 1987.

This is a very thorough discussion accurately described by its title. It covers issues affecting both advanced graduate students and junior faculty members.

Index

This book was set in Baskerville and Eras typefaces. Baskerville was designed by John Baskerville at his private press in Birmingham, England, in the eighteenth century. The first typeface to depart from oldstyle typeface design, Baskerville has more variation between thick and thin strokes. In an effort to insure that the thick and thin strokes of his typeface reproduced well on paper, John Baskerville developed the first wove paper, the surface of which was much smoother than the laid paper of the time. The development of wove paper was partly responsible for the introduction of typefaces classified as modern, which have even more contrast between thick and thin strokes.

Eras was designed in 1969 by Studio Hollenstein in Paris for the Wagner Typefoundry. A contemporary script-like version of a sans-serif typeface, the letters of Eras have a monotone stroke and are slightly inclined.

Printed on acid-free paper.